Twayne's English Authors Series

Sylvia E. Bowman, *Editor*

INDIANA UNIVERSITY

Sir Walter Scott

(TEAS) 39

Sir Walter Scott

By JOHN LAUBER

University of Alberta

Twayne Publishers, Inc. :: New York

To JEAN

SIR WALTER SCOTT

by

JOHN LAUBER

Although Sir Walter Scott was considered for nearly a century one of the greatest, if not the greatest, of British novelists, his reputation has drastically declined during the past fifty years or so. His work has been the object of critical hostility, or (what is probably more damaging in the long run) of indifference and neglect. Because the most recent general study of the novels appeared in 1907, it seems more than time for an analysis and reassessment of his work by modern standards. Biographies of Scott abound, but of criticism—even during the period of his greatest fame—there has been surprisingly little. Scott has remained for too long simply an imposing historical figure. This study, never an attempt to destroy a reputation, intends through the use of modern critical tools to provide an answer to the question—what is the relevance and value of Scott's work TODAY?

Preface

Although Sir Walter Scott's reputation remains high in the standard histories of English literature and of the English novel, it seems safe to say that his work appears to be losing its attraction for both the professional critic and the general reader. Scott has had several modern biographers, but critical and scholarly studies of his poems and novels are surprisingly scarce; in fact, no book-length critical work on his poetry or fiction has been published during the twentieth century. Is this neglect due merely to a change of literary fashions, like that which resulted in the temporary depreciation of Milton and some of the Romantic poets, or to the recognition of radical flaws in his writings? Do his novels speak to us, across the gap of almost a century and a half, as living works of art (like those of his contemporary, Jane Austen), or do they retain interest primarily as part of the history of English and world literature? To such questions this study attempts to provide an answer.

Scott was a complete man of letters—novelist, poet, critic, historian, biographer, editor—and his total production was enormous. His scholarly work, however, although important and valuable in its own time, has been superseded and can be passed over in a comparatively brief study such as this. One chapter is devoted to his poetry and one to his criticism of fiction, which is important both for its intrinsic interest and for its obvious relation to his own fiction. The remainder of this study is devoted to his novels, which form the basis of his permanent reputation.

To write a detailed criticism of each of the thirty-odd Waverley Novels would hardly be practical and, luckily, is unnecessary. The novels selected for consideration—*Waverley, Guy Mannering, The Antiquary, Old Mortality, Rob Roy, The Heart of Midlothian, The Black Dwarf, A Legend of Montrose, Redgauntlet*—are thoroughly representative and are those usually considered his finest. In the conclusion certain characteristics of plot, character, theme, subject and style common to the novels are discussed; the development of Scott criticism is summarized; and the nature and extent of his influence on English and world literature is indicated.

JOHN LAUBER

University of Alberta
Edmonton, Alberta

Contents

Contents

Chronology

1771   August 15, Walter Scott born, at Edinburgh, Scotland.
1772   Suffers from infantile paralysis; left permanently lame.
1773   Sent to grandfather's farm at Sandy-Knowe to recover.
1778   Enters Edinburgh High School.
1783   Enters University of Edinburgh.
1786   Apprenticed in his father's law office.
1792   Admitted to the bar.
1795–
1796   Love affair with Wilhelmina Belsches.
1796   Translations of Bürger's "Lenore" and "Der Wilde Jager."
1798   Marriage to Charlotte Carpenter.
1799   Translation of Goethe's *Goetz von Berlichingen.*
1802–
1803   *Minstrelsy of the Scottish Border.*
1804   Edition of *Sir Tristrem.*
1805   *The Lay of the Last Minstrel.*
1805   Enters secret partnership in Ballantyne printing house.
1808   *Marmion.*
1808   Edition of Dryden's works.
1810   *The Lady of the Lake.*
1813   *The Bridal of Triermain.*
1813   *Rokeby.*
1814   *Waverley.*
1814   Edition of Swift's works.
1814   Visits the Hebrides.
1815   *Guy Mannering.*
1815   Meets Byron; visits Paris after Waterloo.
1815   *The Lord of the Isles.*
1817   *Harold the Dauntless*, Scott's last narrative poem.
1816   *The Antiquary.*

1816   *Tales of My Landlord*, First Series (including *Old Mortality* and *The Black Dwarf*).

1817   Beginning of series of nearly fatal attacks of gallstones, lasting two years.

1818   *Rob Roy*.

1818   *Tales of My Landlord*, Second Series (*The Heart of Midlothian*).

1818   Visited by Washington Irving.

1818   Scott accepts a baronetcy, becomes Sir Walter Scott.

1819   *Tales of My Landlord*, Third Series (*The Bride of Lammermoor* and *A Legend of Montrose*).

1819   *Ivanhoe*.

1820   *The Monastery*.

1820   *The Abbot*.

1820   *Kenilworth*.

1821   *The Pirate*.

1822   Visit of George IV to Edinburgh, stage-managed by Scott.

1822   *The Fortunes of Nigel*.

1823   *Quentin Durward*.

1824   *Redgauntlet*.

1824   Completes a series of critical biographies of English novelists, later collected as *Lives of the Novelists*.

1824   *St. Ronan's Well*.

1826   Financial ruin. Scott devotes remainder of his life to repaying his creditors.

1826   *Woodstock*.

1826   Death of Charlotte Scott.

1826   Visit to France.

1827   *Life of Napoleon*.

1827   *Chronicles of the Canongate*, First Series ("The Highland Widow," "The Two Drovers," and "The Surgeon's Daughter").

1828   *The Fair Maid of Perth*.

1829   *Anne of Geierstein*.

1830   Suffers first stroke.

1831   *Count Robert of Paris*.

1831   *Castle Dangerous*.

1832   Journey to Italy for health; physical and mental collapse. September 21: death at Abbotsford.

Sir Walter Scott

CHAPTER 1

Scott's Literary Career

WALTER SCOTT was born in Edinburgh on August 15, 1771, into a prosperous middle-class family, which still retained close ties with the countryside and the traditions of the Scottish Borders, where the clan of Scotts had been noted for centuries in war, robbery, and feud. The decisive event of his childhood was an attack of infantile paralysis at the age of two, which left him permanently lame because of a shrunken and contracted right leg. In the hope that country air and exercise would restore his health, the child was sent to his grandfather's farm at Smailholme. Here the past retained far more life than in bustling, growing, self-consciously enlightened Edinburgh; and the child learned traditional ballads and stories, many of them concerned with the deeds of his own ancestors. Abundant time for reading allowed him to pursue his interests. Health and vigor were regained as the boy, in spite of his lameness, grew up to become a tireless walker and a lover of every outdoor sport; and his lameness apparently had no such traumatic effect as Lord Byron's club foot. On his return to the city, Scott's education followed the conventional pattern—Edinburgh High School, the University of Edinburgh, training in the law, and finally admission to the bar in 1792.

I First a Poet

Meanwhile, Scott had pursued the interests developed as a child. He read omnivorously—Pope, Dryden, Swift, and Johnson, one assumes, but above all works of romance—Spenser (for the adventures rather than the allegory), *Don Quixote,* and the chivalric romances of Ariosto and Boiardo. He became a famous storyteller among his schoolmates and improvised with a friend endless tales of knight errantry. Above all, Scotland's past absorbed him. As a child, he had learned the Jacobite songs and had become a convert to that lost cause. As a boy, he became acquainted with Stewart of Invernahyle, who had fought in the Jacobite risings of 1715 and 1745, who had lain in hiding for weeks on his own estate after the final defeat at Culloden, who had survived a broadsword duel with the famous highland bandit Rob Roy, and who abounded in stories of Highland life before the clans had been tamed.

Admitted to the bar, Scott practiced with only moderate success, for his interests lay elsewhere. He engaged in an unsuccessful love affair, and made his first experiments in literature. News of the poetry and drama of the German *Sturm und Drang* had just reached Edinburgh; and a group of enthusiastic young men, of whom Scott was one, began the study of the language. The result was the appearance in 1796 of Scott's first published work—translations of the ballads "Lenore" and of "Der Wilde Jäger" by the German poet Bürger—followed in 1799 by a more substantial work, a translation of Goethe's drama, *Götz von Berlichingen.*

None of these works attracted notice. Scott remained a young lawyer who possessed a good deal of leisure for antiquarian studies; for excursions about the country, especially to the Border, to search for ballads and stories; and for the practice of literature as an avocation. Scott had married, but his life was little changed and his relationship with his wife was placid rather than passionate—he never forgot his first love. Meanwhile he was preparing a major work, *The Minstrelsy of the Scottish Border* (1802). The *Minstrelsy* was a collection of Border ballads, forty-three of them previously unpublished, accompanied by lengthy historical annotation. The work now has only historical interest, later scholarship having rendered it obsolete; but it had a decisive influence on Scott's career. He had discovered his proper subject, Scottish history and tradition, and his biographer Lockhart hardly exaggerates in claiming that the *Minstrelsy* was the source of all his later work as poet and novelist.

While the *Minstrelsy* enjoyed a substantial *succès d'estime* and first made Scott's name widely known, it produced only a moderate profit. Then, at the suggestion of a friend, he began *The Lay of the Last Minstrel,* a narrative poem including love, war, and sorcery and with a setting of the medieval Scottish border. Scott's meter, tone, and even occasional phrases were borrowed from

Coleridge's "Christabel," which he had heard recited; but, since "Christabel" remained unpublished for another ten years, the *Lay* produced an effect of complete originality. Its success was immediate and enormous, and Scott became a professional writer. *Marmion,* a narrative poem dealing with sixteenth-century Scotland and describing the disastrous Battle of Flodden, followed in 1808; and its success was even greater. Twenty-five thousand copies were sold within ten years (such sales for a volume of poetry would be remarkable in the 1960's in Great Britain or in America). So high had his reputation risen that his publisher offered him a thousand pounds for the work without having seen a line of it. *The Lady of the Lake* (1810) made the Highlands fashionable and surpassed the sales of the earlier poems. Scott was by this time easily the most famous and successful living poet of Great Britain; but decline quickly set in with the comparative failure of *Rokeby,* a longer, more complex poem with a background of the English civil wars. Scott soon recognized that his vogue was expiring and that his poems could not compete with the exotic backgrounds and gloomy intensity of Byron's *Childe Harold* and Oriental tales, and turned to a different field, the novel.

During these years his energies had not been taken up entirely with poetry. Besides his official duties as Sheriff of Selkirkshire and clerk of the court (which together brought him a handsome income), he had edited, besides a number of minor works, complete editions of Dryden and Swift, each prefaced by a full-length biography. These editions do not meet the requirements of modern scholarship, but they remained standard throughout the century. The choice of subject is a significant indication of Scott's personal tastes and literary principles, which were primarily neo-Classic rather than Romantic, in spite of the superficial romanticism of his subjects and settings.

II *Businessman and Writer*

Scott the lawyer, Scott the editor, and Scott the poet have been considered; and Scott the businessman must not be forgotten since his business career had a profound effect on his life and a considerable one on his work. Scott's biographers assure us that he did not really care for money; but he certainly cared intensely for the things money could buy—land, luxury, social position—and the distinction seems rather difficult to make. He strongly believed that authors were exploited by booksellers and wished to earn for himself *all* the profits—those of author, of publisher, and of printer. Accordingly, he entered into a secret partnership with James Ballantyne, owner of a printing shop in Edinburgh. Secrecy was required because the partnership might have been considered incompatible with Scott's official positions, but he was the dominant partner and controlled every action of Ballantyne. The printinghouse received the contracts to print Scott's works—the many-volumed Dryden and Swift provided plenty of work, and the fact may have induced Scott to undertake the projects—or Scott refused to deal with a publisher. Soon Ballantyne transformed itself into a publishing house, a branch of the business which failed disastrously after a few years because of Scott's bad judgment in choice of publications. It was wound up, but left extensive debts and mountainous piles of unsalable volumes.

It was necessary for Scott either to try a new line or to live on his quite comfortable official income. In this emergency he remembered a fragment of a novel dealing with the Jacobite rebellion of 1745 which he had written ten years before and had given up when discouraged by the comments of friends. (Scott's picturesque story of accidentally discovering the completely forgotten fragment while ransacking an old desk in search of fishing tackle need not be accepted; he was extremely methodical in his literary habits and knew very well the potential value of anything he wrote.) The novel, *Waverley*, was completed, published anonymously in the usual three-decker form, and took the reading public by storm. Sales were unprecedented and the work was read as eagerly in England as in Scotland, in spite of the sometimes nearly impenetrable dialect of its minor characters. Scott had instantly established himself as the great entertainer of his age, admired not only by the general public but by such personages as the Prince Regent—later George IV—and Byron. The pretense of anonymity was retained, partly out of a love of mystification and partly from a shrewd calculation that it helped to maintain interest and therefore sales; but all of Scott's contemporaries who counted were aware of the real identity of the author of *Waverley*. Indeed, no reader of critical discernment, comparing the novels with Scott's acknowledged works, could have seriously doubted his authorship.

Waverley produced immense profits, but Scott's expenditures quickly rose to meet and even to surpass his new income. Obsessed with the dream of founding a landed family—the Scotts of Abbotsford, living in feudal grandeur surrounded by a devoted peasantry—he recklessly bought hundreds of acres of land and turned his simple country house into a sham castle complete with turrets, armor, and carvings in simulated oak (and incongruously provided with the most modern conveniences such as gas lighting and water closets). His profits were great, his expenses were greater, and novel followed novel at an incredible rate. Seven three-volume novels appeared between 1814 and 1820, besides two one-volume works, two long narrative poems, and a great bulk of miscellaneous writing. Such speed, made possible by his refusal to plan or to revise his work, was rendered necessary by constantly mounting expenses. There is much truth in Carlyle's sardonic summary, "Scott's career consisted of writing impromptu novels to buy farms with."

Meanwhile the triumphant progression of the novels continued. Neither business nor Scott's extensive social life nor even an almost fatal illness interrupted them. Too weak to hold a pen, Scott dictated *Rob Roy* and it appeared as scheduled. When, after nine successive stories with a Scottish background, a change of scene appeared desirable, Scott set *Ivanhoe* in the England of Richard Coeur de Lion and was rewarded by his greatest English success. English history was exploited again in *Kenilworth, The Fortunes of Nigel,* and elsewhere. *Quentin Durward* (1823), set in fifteenth century France, again opened new territory and raised Scott's European fame to a level equal with his English reputation. Visitors from the British Isles, from Europe, and from America made the pilgrimage to Abbotsford and were hospitably entertained.

III *Financial Disaster*

Suddenly Scott's ambitions ended in disaster. Early in 1826 his publisher, Constable, and the Ballantyne press went bankrupt. Ironically the collapse occurred only a few months after the long-delayed completion of Abbotsford. Feeling himself morally, although not legally, bound, Scott undertook by his writings to pay a mass of debt totaling well over one hundred thousand pounds. Except for a visit to Paris to gather materials for his life of Napoleon, the remaining years of Scott's life were given to uninterrupted labor; and the works of those years show the pressure under which they were written. By 1831 the debt had been nearly cleared; but the strain had been too great and a sudden collapse, both physical and mental, occurred. After a useless journey to Italy in search of health, Scott returned to die at Abbotsford at the age of sixty-one, on September 21, 1832.

CHAPTER 2

The Poetry

SCOTT'S poetry appears irretrievably faded today. His heroics no longer thrill; his rhetoric seems rant; and his sentiment, sentimentality. His language too often alternates between a rather stilted eighteenth-century poetic diction and obtrusive archaisms designed to lend the proper medieval tone to his work. The long narrative poems on which his poetic reputation rested appear flimsy and unsubstantial in structure, in characterization, and in versification. As a poet, Scott survives today in *The Lady of the Lake* and in "Lochinvar"—high school "standards"—and in a few quotations now losing their familiarity: "Oh, what a tangled web we weave/When first we practice to deceive," "Lives there a man with soul so dead," "a ministering angel thou."

Yet it must be remembered that Scott was a poet for twenty years before he became a novelist; and he continued to be one, if only in the mottoes and songs of the novels, until the end of his career. For a period of six or seven years, from about 1805 to 1812, he was beyond comparison the most widely read and admired of living English poets; and even ten years later it seemed reasonable to Byron, in his dedication to *Don Juan*, to accord Scott supremacy over the Lake Poets: "Scott, Rogers, Campbell, Moore and Crabbe will try/'Gainst thee the question with posterity." The student of Scott, then, cannot ignore his poetry: it gained Scott his fame, it occupied much of his life, and in it may be traced the development of the novelist.

Scott's poetic career began under the influence of the German *Sturm und Drang* with his translations of the popular ballads "Lenore" and "Der Wilde Jäger" of Gottfried Bürger. The best that can be said of them is that they do not fall far below the level of their originals. The influence of Bürger, however, was decisive in Scott's development: it directed his attention toward the ballad style and toward the poetic possibilities of legend and folklore. Less fortunately, it encouraged a taste for the supernatural and "Gothic" which was to mar much of his poetry and several of his novels. Scott was seldom successful in his treatment of the supernatural.

Reinforcing the influence of Bürger was that of the Scottish popular ballads, which Scott enthusiastically collected, and with many of which he had been familiar since childhood. Inevitably, his first original works of any importance, "Glenfinlas" and "The Eve of St. John," were ballad imitations based, like Bürger's work, on legends of terror and the supernatural. Scott, of course, was only one of many poets of the time—Chatterton, Wordsworth, Coleridge, Blake—who escaped from the tradition of Pope to the ballad style. Other imitations followed; although, with only rare exceptions, Scott either could not or did not choose to reproduce the simplicity of diction and complete objectivity of the best traditional ballads.

I *Editor of Ballads*

Again it appears inevitable, in the light of Scott's background and interests, that he should edit a collection of ballads, *Minstrelsy of the Scottish Border* (three volumes 1802–3). Perhaps, too, Scott shrewdly recognized the opportunity to make a name for himself; for, since Bishop Percy's *Reliques of Antient English Poetry*, published thirty years before, ballads had been fashionable. For such a work Scott was peculiarly qualified by study and, perhaps more importantly still, by early association. Scott was a "creative," rather than a scrupulous, editor. His procedure is summarized by H. J. C. Grierson: "Scott composed his texts by a process of combining different versions, correcting and improving the phraseology, the rhythm and the rhyme, heightening . . . the archaic flavour, rewriting and supplying whole stanzas . . ."[1] It has been suggested that he occasionally supplied not only whole stanzas but whole poems, including the famous "Twa Corbies." (If the "Twa Corbies" is really Scott's, it will probably prove his most lasting contribution to English poetry.)

He cannot, however, be fairly judged by standards of scholarship which did not yet exist. Compared to Percy, who was prepared to include in his *Reliques* anything from "Edward" to

Christopher Marlowe's "Come Live with Me and Be My Love"—
if only it were "antient"— Scott seems a scholarly and systematic
editor. Scott divided his material into three classes: historical ballads, "romantic" ballads, and contemporary imitations, many of
them his own, all accompanied by extremely generous commentary. ("Tam Lane," for example, provided him with the occasion
for an eighty-page dissertation on popular superstitions.) It is significant of Scott's interests, always centered in what his age called
"manners," that he appears to be concerned primarily with the
documentary rather than with the poetic value of the ballads. His
lengthy introduction gives more than a hundred pages to Border
life and not one page to the ballads as poetry. Perhaps, indeed, he
did not fully recognize the most distinctive qualities of the ballads: their simplicity of language, their compression of incident,
their perfect objectivity, and their tragic intensity. Such a failure
of understanding is suggested by his comment that modern imitators were able to supply "elegance of sentiment" and a finished
versification which the popular ballads had lacked—and presumably needed. Nevertheless, after all qualifications, the *Minstrelsy*
is a notable work, one of the great ballad collections; and it aided
the survival of such fine poems as "Lord Randal," "Tam Lane,"
"The Wife of Usher's Well, and "The Demon Lover."

II *The Lay of the Last Minstrel*

So scholarly and expensive a work as the *Minstrelsy* could
hardly become a best seller ("It was, on the whole, one of those
books which are more praised than they are read," Scott later observed in his Introduction), but it established its editor's reputation. A kind of sequel, an edition of the medieval romance "Sir
Tristrem," followed in 1804; and Scott, discontented with the
drudgery of the law and by his slow progress in his profession,
and ready for more ambitious original work, was free to follow his
desire to present the "manners" of the ancient Border on a larger
scale than a ballad would permit. Accident provided him with a
subject when the Countess of Dalkeith suggested a ballad dealing
with a Border legend of a goblin page and his malicious pranks. A
second accident provided Scott with his verse form; a friend who
was familiar with the poetry of Wordsworth and Coleridge recited aloud parts of Coleridge's unpublished "Christabel." The

form of "Christabel," Scott remarked in his introduction, "from the singularly irregular structure of the stanzas, and the liberty which it allowed the author to adapt the sound to the sense, seemed exactly suited to such an extravaganza as I meditated." The composition of the *Lay* was thoroughly characteristic of the author in its speed and in its departure from the original plan. When the poem outgrew the original intention of a few stanzas about a goblin page, Scott simply wrote on, with no idea of how the *Lay* was to end. Again—like most of Scott's work—the poem was composed at breakneck speed, a canto a week. The most distinctive feature, the "frame" provided by the aged minstrel who is supposed to be reciting, resulted from the suggestion of friends that some kind of prologue was necessary to place the reader in the proper state of mind. The final result was an extremely confused narrative of Border adventure, war, love, magic, and goblin pranks—with a dash of pathos added in the character of the last minstrel.

Scott had anticipated success, but not the enormous popularity which the *Lay* instantly won. "In the history of British poetry," Lockhart wrote thirty years later, "nothing has ever equaled the demand for 'The Lay of the Last Minstrel' " [2]; and the sales figures support his claim—at least forty-four thousand copies sold before Scott's death. To realize the significance of this figure, one must remember that the combined population of England and Scotland in 1805 was scarcely more than one-twentieth of that of the United States today; moreover, a large fraction of the population must also have been illiterate. Such a sale indicates that the early ninteenth century, unlike the twentieth, was a poetry-reading age. The figures, however, are somewhat misleading; and the comparison is not quite so much to the disadvantage of the present as it might seem. The popular poetry of the time—whether by Scott, or Byron, or Crabbe, or Moore,—was narrative poetry that was usually neither subtle nor complex and was nearly as easy to read as a novel (much easier than the best modern novels). More original and difficult works, such as the poems of Wordsworth or Keats, sold by the hundred or the dozen rather than by the thousand. Scott's public was the entertainment-seeking public which today is amused by the best-selling novel, television, or the motion picture. The audience for difficult poetry may have been no larger, proportionately, in 1805 or 1810 than in 1965.

The obvious faults of structure were recognized, and freely admitted by the author; but the public was indifferent to the fact that the goblin page had become, in Scott's word, an "excrescence," and that the whole sixth canto, containing a description of the festivities at the wedding of the hero and heroine and the songs of the minstrels, was unnecessary. Scott ingenuously explained the existence of the canto in a letter to a friend: "the poem should certainly have closed with the union of the lovers, when the interest, if any, was at an end. But what could I do? I had my book and my page still on my hands, and must get rid of them at all events. Manage them as I would, their catastrophe must have been insufficient to occupy an entire canto; so I was fain to eke it out with the songs of the minstrels." [3]

Readers, however, were entranced by the apparent novelty of subject and form; and they agreed with Jeffrey in his review of the *Lay* that "delightful images and affecting sentiments" were more important than unity or coherence. Luckily, too, "Christabel" was unavailable for comparison. Indeed, the reminiscences of "Christabel" are striking. One may compare the openings: " 'Tis the middle of night by the castle clock/And the owls have awakened the crowing cock" (Coleridge); "The feast was over in Branksome tower,/And the ladye had gone to her secret bower" (Scott). A more striking similarity exists between Coleridge's description of Christabel's entry into her father's castle with Geraldine and Scott's account of his heroine stealing forth at night to meet her lover.

Christabel:

> The mastiff old did not awake,
> Yet she an angry moan did make!
>
> . . . .
>
> They passed the hall, that echoes still,
> Pass as lightly as you will!
> The brands were flat, the brands were dying,
> Amid their own white ashes lying:
>
> . . . .

They steal their way from stair to stair,
Now in glimmer and now in gloom,
And now they pass the Baron's room
As still as death, with stifled breath!

The Lay:

Why does she stop and look often around,
  As she glides down the secret stair;
And why does she pat the shaggy bloodhound,
  As he rouses him up from his lair;
And, though she passes the postern alone,
Why is not the watchman's bugle blown?
The ladye steps in doubt and dread
Lest her watchful mother hear her tread;
The ladye caresses the rough bloodhound
Lest his voice should waken the castle round;

Coleridge was justifiably disturbed, not so much by the obvious plagiarism—Scott is not saved by the fact that his heroine is leaving a castle while Coleridge's is entering one—as by the manner in which Scott coarsened the passage, making language and meter heavy and obvious. The subtleties of the "Christabel" meter were beyond Scott's capacity, and by Canto III the poem settles fairly consistently into the rather irregular iambic tetrameter couplets that became typical of his longer poems. Modern readers will probably agree with Grierson that "in the best of the ballads, say 'Tamlane' and 'The Twa Corbies,' there is more of imaginative poetry than in the whole of *The Lay.*" [4]

I Marmion

With the publication of the *Lay*, literature rather than the law became Scott's profession. So brilliant a success demanded a sequel, but Scott was delayed by the variety of literary tasks which he had undertaken; as a result, *Marmion* did not appear until 1808. The author intended, the Advertisement announced, "to paint the manners of the feudal times upon a broader scale, and in the course of a more interesting story" than in the *Lay*. The frame provided in his earlier poem by passages dealing with the last minstrel was replaced by a series of introductory epistles—one preceding each canto—describing the scenery and seasons of

Ashetiel, Scott's residence at the time of writing, and containing the author's meditations on poetry and many other subjects. It was thoroughly characteristic of Scott that these verse-letters, which now seem the most attractive part of *Marmion,* were originally composed quite without reference to that poem. They were first intended to appear independently as "Six Epistles from Ettrick Forest."

The poem reaches its climax with the great national disaster of Flodden, fought in 1513, in which almost the entire Scottish army, including King James IV and most of his nobility, was annihilated by the English. The narrative, however, is concerned primarily with the adventures of purely fictitious characters whose fates are determined by the outcome of the historical battle (a method which was to be typical of Scott's historical fiction). Lord Marmion, a favorite of Henry VIII, journeys to Scotland to inquire about the warlike preparations of King James. Marmion has previously sought the hand of the beautiful Clara de Clare, a wealthy heiress, who is in love with Ralph de Wilton. Marmion disposes of his rival by forging a letter implicating him in treason, then by overthrowing him in single combat during a trial by battle. Clara de Clare takes refuge in a nunnery. De Wilton, who survives the fight, wanders the world disguised as a palmer and finally returns just in time to guide Marmion (who, of course, does not recognize him) to Edinburgh. Meanwhile, wishing to be free to marry Clara, Marmion has betrayed his mistress, Constance de Beverley, whom he had stolen from a convent. In punishment for violating her oath of chastity, Constance is immured alive; but, before the sentence is carried out, she produces documents proving de Wilton's innocence. After further complications which need not be detailed, Marmion is killed at Flodden and de Wilton is united with Clara. Marmion's death provides the occasion for two of the most quoted passages in Scott's poetry: the dying man's exclamation "O what a tangled web we weave/When we first practice to deceive!" and the apostrophe to woman—"A ministering angel thou/When pain and anguish wring the brow"—which is delivered as Clara, forgetting the injuries he has done her, brings water to Marmion.

Francis Jeffrey's criticisms in the *Edinburgh Review* that the plot is excessively improbable because of Scott's reliance on chance and coincidence; that it is overly complicated and clumsily explained; and that it contains actions inconsistent with character, such as Marmion's forgery of the letter, seem thoroughly justified. Jeffrey added that he found "a great deal too much gratuitous description," a charge confirmed by Scott's admission that he brought Marmion to Edinburgh by an impossible route simply to give himself a pretext for describing certain scenery.

Descriptions of nature formed one of the principal attractions of both the poems and the novels for Scott's contemporaries; but a brief comparison with Wordsworth is enough to reveal the decorative, nonfunctional, and essentially conventional character of Scott's descriptions. By this time, incidentally, Scott was personally acquainted with Wordsworth and knew his poetry. A rather obvious reminiscence of Wordsworth's "Solitary Reaper," is seen in Scott's Canto III

> A mellow voice Fitz-Eustace had,
> The air he chose was wild and sad;
> Such have I heard in Scottish land
> Rise from the busy harvest band,
> When falls before the mountaineer
> On Lowland plains the ripened ear,
> Now one shrill voice the notes prolong,
> Now a wild chorus swells the song:
> Oft have I listened and stood still
> As it came softened up the hill,
> And deemed it the lament of men
> Who languished for their native glen.

Scott's lines lack the imaginative power and poignance of Wordsworth's poem:

> Behold her, single in the field,
> Yon solitary Highland lass!
> Reaping and singing by herself;
> Stop here, or gently pass!
> Alone she cuts and binds the grain,
> And sings a melancholy strain;
> O listen! for the Vale profound
> Is overflowing with the sound.

Nowhere does Scott reveal his own poetic limitations more clearly than in such echoes of greater poets.

As was to become usual in Scott's works, the official hero and heroine are the faintest shadows, with the result that no reader can take much interest in whether Clara will be forced to marry Marmion or how De Wilton will regain his reputation. Marmion is interesting as the first complete "Byronic" hero in English literature, at a time when Byron had published nothing but *Hours of Idleness*. Like Byron's heroes, Marmion is dark, haughty, and haunted by guilt; but, unlike Byron, Scott makes the mistake of explicitly defining the hero's crime. The flaw is not in the inappropriateness of forgery to the period of the poem but in the sordidness of the act and its practical, mercenary motive—desire to marry a wealthy heiress. Of the historical characters, James IV, the king whose rashness ruins his country, has interesting potentialities. Like Marmion, he feels guilt (for the death of his father) and alternately punishes himself and seeks forgetfulness through love, festivity, or war. But James appears at length in only one canto.

The weaknesses of the poem were obvious; but public response equaled that to the *Lay* and totally disproved Jeffrey's prophecy in his review of the *Lay* that "Mr. Scott must either sacrifice his Border prejudices, or offend all his readers in the other parts of the empire." Scott's friend George Ellis assured him that *Marmion* was to be placed "on the very top shelf of English poetry" [5] with Dryden's "Theodore and Honoria." One contemporary remained immune to the enchantment. Wordsworth, in a letter to Scott, remarked dryly that "I think your end has been attained. That it is not the end which I should wish you to propose to yourself, you will be well aware." [6] But Scott could finish his introduction to *Marmion* in the collected edition of his works by complacently noting that "the return of sales before me makes the copies amount to thirty-six thousand printed between 1808 and 1825."

III Lady of the Lake

The Lady of the Lake (1810) achieved perhaps the greatest popularity of all. As reported by a contemporary, suspense was aroused long before the poem's appearance, as James Ballantyne, the printer, read cantos aloud to selected hearers: "Common fame

was loud in their favor; a great poem was on all hands anticipated. I do not recollect that any of all the author's works was
ever looked for with more intense anxiety, or that any of them
excited a more extraordinary sensation when it did appear. The
whole country rang with the praises of the poet—crowds set off to
view the scenery of Loch Katrine, till then comparatively unknown; . . . and every house and inn in that neighborhood was
crammed with a constant succession of visitors." [7] Ever since its
publication, *The Lady of the Lake* has been the most frequently
reprinted of the longer poems.

As with its two predecessors, the historical background is that
of pre-Reformation Scotland; but this time the action occurs
largely in the Highlands rather than on the Border. The distinctive peculiarities of the *Lay* and *Marmion* reappear. The insignificance of the official hero, Malcolm Graeme, who completely disappears during the greater part of the poem, was confessed by
Scott: "I gave him that dip in the lake by way of making him do
something. But wet or dry I could make nothing of him. His insignificance is the greatest defect among many others in the poem;
but the canvas was not broad enough to include him, considering
I had to group the king, Roderick, and Douglas." [8] As in the *Lay*,
the final canto is superfluous. It presents the battle between Highlanders and Lowlanders which ought to have formed the climax
of the poem, but, in Scott's words, "all the principal characters
had been disposed of before it came on, and were absent at the
time of action, and nothing hinged upon the issue." [9] But the public was delighted by the picturesque scenery of the Highlanders
and the still more picturesque costumes and manners of the Highlanders.

One dissent, at least, was registered in private by the best critic
of the time, Coleridge, in a letter written to Wordsworth shortly
after reading the first two cantos. Coleridge complained of the
slowness of movement, both of verse and of action: "I never remember a narrative poem in which I felt the sense of Progress so
languid," and was rewarded only by two or three "pleasing Images." He then proposed a formula for such poems:

The first business must be, a vast string of Patronymics, and names of
Mountains, Rivers, etc.—the most commonplace imagery . . . look al-

poems and in Scott's introductions, but it seems to mean little more than "picturesque," or else "lacking in organization and artistic discipline." Such deficiencies he elevated into virtues: "Then wild as cloud, or stream, or gale,/Flow on, flow unconfined, my tale!" (*Marmion,* Introduction to Canto III). The most distinctive aspects of Romanticism—the concept of poetry as expression rather than imitation, the emphasis on the power of the imagination, the organic concept of art—cannot be found in Scott's work. He simply was not interested in such, to him, fanciful speculations. His own taste, except for his love of ballads, was thoroughly conservative and neo-classic. His favorite poems were Samuel Johnson's "London" and "The Vanity of Human Wishes," and the highly conservative George Crabbe was the contemporary whom he most admired. The gap which existed between the early Wordsworth and the public did not exist for Scott.

The apparent striking originality of his poetry is really superficial. It is true that no narrative poems quite like them had previously appeared, but their debt to the Gothic novel is obvious. Coleridge's charge that Scott had versified the Gothic clichés of character and situation seems largely justified, although many of Scott's situations, like the lovers belonging to hostile families in the *Lay* or the king in disguise in *The Lady of the Lake,* are of course much older. Verse, together with the Highland or Border settings, lent a superficial novelty which sustained them for a few years. By accident Scott had hit on an essential part of the formula for popular success; his narrative poems were entertainingly novel without being disturbingly original. No doubt, too, his easy sentimentality helped:

> The tear, down Childhood's cheek that flows,
> Is like the dewdrop on the rose;
> When next the summer breeze comes by,
> And waves the bush, the flower is dry.   (*Rokeby,* IV)

The poems were rapidly written (poetry is "very little labour," Scott remarked) and were intended to be rapidly and uncritically read. For such reading, it is enough if the author simply names the poetic objects—bards, knights, ladies, castles, crags, swords, spears. Poetry of this kind is completely dependent on the reader's stock response to standard "poetic" and "romantic" properties. "To form an estimate of Scott's poetry," Coleridge remarked, it would be necessary to "take away all his names of old castles, which rhyme very prettily, and read very picturesquely; then . . . all the old armour and weapons; next I would exclude the mention of all nunneries, abbeys, and priories, and then I should see what would be the residuum—how much poetry would remain." [12] Very little, is the clear implication.

Nor does the language of the poetry, from line to line, bear analysis. Scott is generally satisfied with the approximate word rather than the exact one, he constantly sacrifices meaning to rhyme, he relies on neo-classic clichés of diction and personification. *Marmion* (Introduction to Canto II) offers a good example: "For Fate shall thrust you from the shore/And Passion ply the sail and oar." A Johnsonian critic might inquire how one "plies" a sail and whether Passion is to be imagined as simultaneously rowing and blowing, as both wind and crew. Another result of Scott's haste is frequent cacophony and awkwardness of syntax—"Him listed ease his battle steed." A more extended example of this syntactical disorder is:

> And then of humour kind and free
> And bearing him to each degree
> With frank and fearless courtesy,
> There never youth was formed to steal
> Upon the heart like brave O'Neale.   (*Rokeby*, IV)

Doggerel of this kind forms a substantial portion of Scott's verse. One objects to such passages not because they violate the conventions of English grammar, but because the violation serves no poetic purpose and seems merely the result of hasty writing and of lack of revision.

This estimate of Scott's poetry is certainly strikingly different from the conventional estimate of the past, of which Grierson's summary may be taken as representative: "Has any poetry, since Shakespeare, making allowances for all the differences in depth of insight and wealth of expression and rhythm, given so much the impression of a bubbling spring of original creative power?" But when one makes those allowances, what is left? On a more concrete level, the most that Grierson can claim is that "Scott is at his best in describing rapid movement, especially the movement of large bodies of men and horse." [13] The narrative poems are of interest principally in foreshadowing the themes and character types of Scott's novels. " 'Proud Maisie' and one or two other poems in the Scottish ballad manner are Scott's contribution to poetry," [14] a recent critic has observed. And this judgment seems borne out by the fact that during the past fifty years or so most critics of English poetry have neither praised nor condemned Scott—they have ignored him.

CHAPTER 3

Scott on the Art of Fiction

ALTHOUGH Scott devoted only a fraction of his effort to criticism, and only a fraction of his criticism to the novel, even that surpasses—in both quantity and importance—the work of any previous or contemporary critic of fiction. His published criticism is found in a variety of locations: in reviews of current novels for the *Quarterly Review*, the *Edinburgh*, and *Blackwood's;* in the series of critical biographies prefaced to the British Novelists series and later collected as *Lives of the Novelists;* and in the prefaces and introductions to his own novels. His journal and his letters provide informal comments on his contemporaries and, together with the introductions to the novels, illustrate the relation between his critical principles and his own practice as a creative writer.

I *Fiction—a Luxury*

Basic to both criticism and practice is Scott's opinion of the novel as a minor form of literature; it is "a mere elegance, a luxury contrived for the amusement of polished life and the gratification of that half-love of literature which pervades all ranks in an advanced state of society." [1] He defends it against the attack of moralists by denying it significance. The function of the novel is to offer "solace from the toils of ordinary life by an excursion into the regions of imagination"; it is a drug, harmful to the addict, but "of most blessed power in those moments when the whole head is sore and the whole heart sick" (*Lives*, 308).

The natural consequence of this attitude is an indifference toward the artistic qualities of the novel that is abundantly revealed by Scott's own methods of work. *Guy Mannering* was "the work of six weeks at Christmas." [2] "Before and after dinner I finished about twenty printed pages of *Woodstock*," [3] and in fifteen days "with intervention of some days idleness, to let imagination brood on the task a little," [4] Scott completed a volume. Such speed allowed, of course, neither planning nor revision. Finishing the second volume (of three) of *Woodstock*, Scott found himself without the slightest idea of how the story was to be concluded, and remarked "I never could lay down a plan—or, having laid it down, I never could adhere to it. . . . I only tried to make that which I was actually writing diverting and interesting, leaving the rest to fate." [5] In prose and verse, Scott habitually composed at top speed. Verse was rewritten once, or occasionally twice; but, after finishing a page of the manuscript of a novel, Scott never looked at it again until he read the proof.

Scott appears to see himself not as an artist but as a craftsman supplying a luxury product, demand for which might cease without warning at any moment. His comment on the comparative failure of his narrative poem "Lord of the Isles"—"Since one line has failed, we must just stick to something else" [6]—suggests a manufacturer withdrawing an obsolescent product in order to replace it with a new model. To vary the metaphor, his novels were the bricks with which Abbotsford was built. He laments in his journal, shortly after the crash of Ballantyne and Constable and his own financial ruin, "I can no longer have the delight of waking in the morning with bright ideas in my mind, haste to commit them to paper, and count them monthly, as the means of planting such groves, and purchasing such wastes." [7] Like a good showman, Scott constantly sought for novelty—Highlanders, Covenanters, Crusaders, fifteenth-century France, Anglo-Norman England—until only one source remained: "to depend for success on the interest of a well-contrived story. But woe's me! That requires thought, consideration, the writing out of a regular plan or plot," [8] of which he believed himself incapable.

For the public which consumed the output of his literary production line, Scott felt a certain contempt. The public, he remarks in his journal, after completing *Anne of Geierstein,* is amused with "rattles and gingerbread" and cannot discriminate: "I should deal very uncandidly with those who may read my confessions were I to say I knew a public worth caring for. . . . Get a good name and you may write trash. Get a bad one and you may write like Homer, without pleasing a single reader." [9]

II *Criticism*

Works produced in such a way—for Scott seems to have assumed that most novelists wrote as he did—for the diversion of such a public would hardly deserve very serious or detailed study. As a result, Scott's criticism is usually descriptive and impressionistic rather than analytical. Thus, after praising in general terms the plot of *Tom Jones* (in his life of Fielding), instead of analyzing its construction, Scott falls back on simile (a favorite device in his criticism) to suggest its effect on the reader, who "glides down the narrative like a boat on the surface of some broad navigable stream, which only winds enough to gratify the voyager with the varied beauty of its banks" (*Lives*, 18–19).

His critical method in his reviews is fairly standardized, and his review of Jane Austen's *Emma* may be considered typical. He begins with a brief discussion of the novel as a literary form, deriving it from the romance (a term not defined); then he distinguishes two types of novel on the basis of their differing degrees of realism. "The novel as formerly composed" was characterized by improbability of action and exaggeration of sentiment; but a new class of fiction has appeared "which draws the characters and incidents introduced more immediately from the current of ordinary life than was permitted by the former rules of the novel," [10] and to this class *Emma* belongs. This preliminary placing of a work in its particular kind of genre is characteristic of Scott and, of course, is also typically neo-classic.

With *Emma* properly classified, Scott discusses its general merits: "the force of a narrative conducted with much neatness and point, and a quiet yet comic dialogue, in which the characters of the speakers evolve themselves with dramatic effect." [11] He praises the characterization, dialogue, and description; but he says nothing about the structure of the book beyond remarking that it has almost no story—Scott apparently conceives of a "story" as a series of physical adventures. He nevertheless summarizes the plot at length and concludes condescendingly, "Such is the simple plan of a story which we peruse with pleasure, if not with deep interest." [12]

His review of *Frankenstein* begins in a similar manner, with a distinction between novels which "bound the events they narrate by the actual laws of nature, and such as, passing these limits, are managed by marvellous and supernatural machinery." Works presenting the "marvellous" are further subdivided into three classes: those written in a time when there was genuine belief in the supernatural and miraculous; those which present supernatural events merely for their sensational effect; and finally a "more philosophical and refined" class "in which the laws are represented as altered . . . in order to show the probable effect which the supposed miracles would produce on those who witnessed them." [18] *Frankenstein* is placed in this third class; and the remainder of the review consists, as was usual in periodical criticism of his time, of lengthy quotations and summary.

The Lives of the Novelists is obviously modeled on Johnson's *Lives of the Poets* and has a similar pattern: a biographical sketch, in which the author's principal works are taken in chronological order and briefly described, is followed by a general criticism. Although intended as biographical criticism, the *Lives* seldom attempts to relate the personality of an author to his work beyond occasional indications of how his experiences provided him with subject matter. The selection of writers seems less arbitrary than in Johnson's series; all of the major eighteenth-century novelists, with the rather surprising exception of Defoe, are included, as well as most of the minor figures. The plan apparently excluded active contemporaries.

Scott is anything but a systematic or theoretical critic; but the principles underlying his criticism can be pieced together from comments, judgments, and occasional brief general discussions scattered through his work. The basic concept of literature is firmly neo-classic: literature is an imitation of life. Scott actually uses the term "imitation" in his prefatory remark that *St. Ronan's Well* "is intended to give the imitation of the shifting manners of our time." The novel is distinguished from the earlier romance primarily by the closeness of its imitation, which produces a unique illusion of reality: "by the circumstantial detail of minute, trivial, and even uninteresting circumstances, the author gives to his fiction an air of reality that can scarcely otherwise be obtained" (*Lives*, 252).

Tom Jones is described, therefore, as the first English novel because it was the first work of fiction "founded upon the plan of painting from nature. Even Richardson's novels are but a step from the old romance . . . dealing in improbable incidents and in characters swelled out beyond the ordinary limit of humanity," whereas *Tom Jones* is "truth and human nature itself" (*Lives*, 18). But Scott is frequently inconsistent—Richardson is later given essentially the same praise. Scott anticipates the observation of Ian Watt that "formal realism," the convention that "the novel is a full and authentic report of human experience, and is therefore under an obligation to satisfy its reader with such details of the story as the individuality of the actors concerned, the particulars of the times and places of their actions, details which are presented through a more largely referential use of language than is common in other literary forms," [14] is the primary and distinctive convention of the novel.

References to "nature," that universal term of neo-classic criticism, appear frequently in his criticism. Scott shared the neo-classic belief in a universal human nature underlying all superficial differences of nation and period—with the significant difference that, while the neo-classic critic looked for this universal nature in civilized and educated man, Scott believed it was most clearly displayed in a barbarous state of society. Logically, Scott frequently expresses the neo-classic preference for the universal and typical over the particular; one may safely assume that he agreed with Johnson's observation that "Nothing can please many, and please long, but just representations of general nature." In his introduction to *The Monastery* Scott explains the failure of one character, the Euphuist Sir Percy Shafton, because of its extreme artificiality. The character consisted entirely of "factitious and affected" qualities, "superinduced on that which was common to the race." On the other hand, the reader's interest is held by James Fenimore Cooper's backwoodsmen and Indians because "the manners of a rude people are always founded on nature, and therefore, the feelings of a more polished generation immediately sympathize with them." Thus, likewise, the polished audience of London or of Edinburgh could sympathize with Scott's Highlanders.

From these critical premises, a concern with subject matter and an indifference toward technique are logical consequences, and both characterize Scott's criticism. Subject matter is regarded as an independent quality; it is able to give value to a work regardless of the manner in which it is rendered by the novelist. Thus in his introduction to *Waverley*, Scott apologizes for the awkward plan of the work on the ground that it allowed him "to introduce at length some descriptions of scenery and manners, to which the reality gave an interest which the powers of the Author might have otherwise failed to attain for them."

Scott's prefaces to his own novels contain little discussion of his artistic intentions or of the technical problems encountered; instead, they are concerned principally with informing the reader of the historical incidents and figures upon which the novels are based; for Scott believed that his work derived its interest and value from its factual accuracy.

It is to be expected, then, that Scott's criticism would be at its weakest in dealing with the technique of the novelist. Of style Scott has almost nothing to say beyond such vague phrases as "uniformly elegant" or "finely written." Wishing to praise the style of *Frankenstein*, he can only say that the book is written in "plain and forcible English" without the "hyperbolical Germanisms" common to its type.[15] The famous plot of *Tom Jones* is commended for its "felicitous contrivance and happy extrication" (*Lives*, 18), and Scott hastens on to discuss the characters. Richardson is praised for his refusal to alter the "noble plan" (*Lives*, 234) of *Clarissa Harlowe* and provide his readers with a happy ending—an example of artistic integrity in sharp contrast with Scott's willingness to alter the conclusion of *St. Ronan's Well* so as to satisfy Ballantyne's fear of impropriety although Scott recognized that the result was to "perplex and weaken the course of his narrative, and the dark effect of its catastrophe." [16] The speed with which his own novels were written, and their unparalleled popularity in spite of their slovenliness of style and construction, might easily have convinced Scott that technique was unimportant in comparison with subject and character. Indeed, Scott seems to have believed that his own improvisation was typical, as his comment about Fielding indicates. Refusing to explain Fielding's failure as a dramatist by his "careless haste," Scott adds: "Neither are we at all disposed to believe that an author so careless . . . took much more pains in labouring his novels than in composing his plays" (*Lives*, 5). But the briefest analysis of *Tom*

Jones would have shown Scott that it must have been labored over a great deal more than any of his own works. Perhaps as a rationalization of his own practice, Scott transformed carelessness into a virtue, holding that "to write much and with abundant spontaneity is better than to polish minutely," [17] that this abundance and spontaneity distinguish all great writers, and that these qualities can be destroyed by excessive care in composition. Thus, whereas Fielding's novels are "free, bold and true sketches," Richardson's are like "paintings which have been very minutely laboured, and, amid their excellence, still exhibit some of the heaviness which almost always attends the highest degree of finishing" (*Lives*, 250).

Although Scott himself was praised for the dramatic qualities of his work ("His stories are digested into scenes, and they often differ from plays only in that the stage-directions, instead of being degraded into the margin, are wrought into sentences"),[18] he had no conception of the importance of the scene. In a discussion of the differences between novel and drama in the life of Fielding— probably the longest theoretical discussion occurring in the *Lives of the Novelists*—Scott explains Fielding's failure as a playwright by observing that "Description and narration, which form the very essence of the novel, must be very sparingly introduced into dramatic composition,"; and that the dramatist, aided by actors and scenery, should be concise, whereas the style of the novelist must be "expanded and circumstantial" (*Lives*, 6–7). The possibility that Fielding's dramatic experience might have aided him in the plotting of *Tom Jones* and in the construction of its scenes apparently escaped Scott.

Scott's fullest treatment of plot is found in his preface to *The Monastery*, in which he explains the severe criticism which that novel received by his awkward handling of the supernatural; the character of Sir Percy Shafton the Euphuist; and the "inartificial" arrangement of the incidents. Although a story made up of disconnected incidents and characters might be defended on the basis of truth to nature—as well as by the example of such writers as Le Sage and Smollett—Scott admits in his preface to *The Monastery* that something more is required of the novelist than "a mere compliance with the simplicity of reality; just as we demand from a scientific gardener that he shall arrange in curious knots and artificial parterres, the flowers which 'nature boon' distributes freely on hill and dale." This significant analogy is based on the formal garden of the seventeenth and early eighteenth centuries, which even Pope has rejected in favor of a more "natural" style; and it reveals the conservatism of Scott's tastes and his distance from the organic concept of art which forms a common denominator of Romantic criticism. The passage presents an absolute form-content dichotomy, with plot serving merely as an embellishment (or distortion) of "simple reality" demanded by a sophisticated taste. Plot is frequently described by Scott as "artificial"; for him, the life and truth of a novel lay in its characters.

Scott's criticism is consistently pragmatic, not only in its lack of a theoretical dimension but also in the sense given to the term by Meyer Abrams of criticism which "looks at the work of art chiefly as a means to an end, an instrument for getting something done, and tends to judge its value according to its success in achieving that aim." [19] In neo-classic theory the purpose of literature is to please and to instruct. Scott consistently emphasizes pleasure, or amusement; but as to whether the novel should, or can, give moral instruction, he is undecided and inconsistent. At times he simply denies moral significance to the novel. He admits Robert Bage's didactic novels to the British Novelists series, despite their radical political and sexual principles, because he considers these "speculative errors" unimportant: "We are far from being of opinion that the youngest and most thoughtless derive their serious principles from works of this nature" (*Lives*, 275). The moral of a work of fiction, Scott remarks in his life of Fielding, is usually ignored by the reader; and "we are inclined to think the worst evil to be apprehended from the perusal of novels is, that the habit is apt to generate an indisposition to real history and useful literature, and that the best which can be hoped is that they may sometimes instruct the youthful mind by real pictures of life, and sometimes awaken their better feelings . . . by strains of generous sentiments and tales of fictitious woe" (*Lives*, 21).

At times Scott approaches a more subtle conception of the nature of morality in fiction, for he occasionally recognizes that it depends not on an appropriate distribution of prizes and punishments in the final chapter but on the manner in which characters and events are treated and the attitudes aroused toward them in the reader: "If our feelings are in favor of virtue, the novel is virtuous; if of vice, the novel is vicious" (*Lives*, 228). Such a concept might have produced a more sophisticated criticism, but Scott's application of it is shallow and conventional. Comparing Voltaire and Johnson as novelists, he declares "The one is a fiend —a merry devil, we grant—who scoffs at and derides human miseries; the other, a friendly though grave philosopher, who shows us the nothingness of earthly hopes, to teach us that our affections ought to be placed elsewhere" (*Lives*, 161). Although Sterne is condemned for indecency and indecorum, Scott finds that *Tristram Shandy* is saved by the character of Uncle Toby, for which the author should be praised "as one who has exalted and honored humanity, and impressed upon his readers such a lively picture of kindness and benevolence . . . that their hearts must be warmed by whenever it is recalled to memory" (*Lives*, 133).

But the reader's pleasure always remains for Scott the primary aim of the novelist. The principal source of this pleasure is the accuracy of the novel's imitation of life, and the success of the novelist lies in revealing universal nature beneath the ephemeral manners of the period he describes. But Scott was not a naturalist, and realism alone could not satisfy him—"something more than a mere signpost likeness is demanded." [20] To describe that "something more," he could find only such vague phrases as "spirit and character" or "depth of knowledge and dexterity of execution" (*Lives*, 193). Once he identifies this necessary quality as imagination: "Every successful novelist must be more or less of a poet. . . . The quality of imagination is absolutely indispensable to him . . ." (*Lives*, 68). But one must not confuse Scott's definition of imagination with Coleridge's; the context of the quotation makes the non-romantic meaning of the term clear. Indeed, to illustrate this poetic power, Scott cites the novels of Smollett.

Scott does not theorize on the nature of imagination, but apparently it is not, for him, a profoundly creative force. Instead, it is limited, in the eighteenth-century sense, to the faculty of association. "Imagination," "fancy," and "invention" are synonymous terms in Scott's criticism; and their power is restricted by the necessity of following "nature" and by the limitations of the human mind. It is not surprising that Scott's concept of originality, or "novelty," to use his customary term, is superficial. Novelty is essential to arouse the reader's interest, but it can be attained by the use of an unfamiliar setting or by the invention of a surprising series of adventures. It is not essential to artistic success, and it may even destroy the integrity of a novel: "It is perhaps not possible, at the same time, to preserve consistency and probability, and attain the interest of novelty." [21] When faced with such a choice, Scott himself sacrificed consistency and probability.

With all of its limitations of theory, however, Scott's criticism is remarkably flexible in application and catholic in taste—qualities rare in the partisan and dogmatic periodical criticism of the time. In his review of Godwin's *Fleetwood,* Scott subjects the book to ridicule; but his condemnation is based on Godwin's literary deficiencies rather than on his radicalism. This review is exceptional, for in general Scott preferred not to criticize if he could not praise. Nonetheless, his judgments of the major novelists of the eighteenth century agree essentially with those still held. Fielding is "the first of British novelists" (*Lives,* 4), and *Tom Jones* is "the most masterly example of an artful and well-told novel" (*Lives,* 68). Smollett, rather surprisingly, is ranked with Fielding, partly because Scott could not consider the formlessness of his novels as a serious defect, and partly, no doubt, merely from national sympathy. Richardson is a writer obviously less congenial, but Scott declares that "The power of Richardson's painting in his deeper scenes of tragedy never has been, and probably never will be, excelled" (*Lives,* 255). Sterne is condemned for affectation: "All popularity thus founded carries in it the seeds of decay; for eccentricity in composition . . . is sure to be caricatured by stupid imitators, to become soon unfashionable, and of course to be neglected" (*Lives,* 130).

The power of rousing strong emotion is, for Scott, one of the major requirements of a novelist; for this reason he gives surprisingly high praise to a sentimentalist like Henry Mackenzie, and to the leading Gothic novelists, Horace Walpole and Ann Radcliffe. To Walpole's *Castle of Otranto* Scott ascribes the power traditionally reserved for tragedy: that of exciting "the passions of fear and pity" (*Lives,* 196). Ann Radcliffe was "the first to introduce into her prose fictions a tone of fanciful description and impressive narrative which had hitherto been exclusively applied to poetry. Fielding, Richardson, Smollett . . . are decidedly prose authors.

Mrs. Radcliffe has a title to be considered as the first poetess of romantic fiction, that is, if actual rhythm shall not be deemed essential to poetry" (*Lives,* 305). This "poetry" apparently lay in the intense feelings of fear and horror which her novels aroused, and in her elaborate, emotionally charged descriptions of scenery.

In dealing with her work, Scott's catholicity of taste approaches a complete relativism. He classifies her novels as melodramas and points out that they gain their interest solely by the creation of fear and suspense: "the force of the production lies, therefore, in the delineation of external incident, while the characters of the agents . . . are entirely subordinate to the scenes in which they are placed," and are mere stereotypes. Scott proceeds to list the stock characters of the Gothic novel: "A dark and tyrannical count; an aged crone of a housekeeper, the depositary of many a family legend; a garrulous waitingmaid; a gay and light-hearted valet; a villain or two of all-work; and a heroine . . . subjected to all manners of hazards, form the stock-in-trade of a romancer or a melodramatist; and if these personages be dressed in the proper costume, and converse in language sufficiently appropriate to their stations and qualities, it is not to be expected that the audience shall shake their sides at the humour of the dialogue, or weep over its pathos" (*Lives,* 320–21). Then Scott defends Mrs. Radcliffe's works (and by implication the Gothic novel in general) by arguing that the question is not "whether the romances of Mrs. Radcliffe possess merits which her plan did not require . . . nor whether hers is to be considered as a department of fictitious composition, equal in dignity and importance to those where the great ancient masters have long preoccupied the ground" (*Lives,* 323), but whether, as melodramas, they are effective. And Scott adds that her novels appeal to a wider audience than those of Richardson or Fielding.

Although Scott reviewed Jane Austen's *Emma,* as a critic of contemporary fiction he dealt principally with the work of minor writers—John Galt, William Godwin, Charles Maturin, James Morier, Mary Shelley (he greatly admired *Frankenstein*). On the whole his judgments of his contemporaries seem remarkably accurate and objective; he is not influenced either by great differences from his own practice in subject and technique, or by obvious imitation of himself—as in Cooper's work. He never reviewed a

Cooper novel, but several references in his letters and his journal reveal interest in Cooper's writings. *The Pilot,* he writes to a friend, is very clever and "the sea-scenes and characters in particular are admirably drawn; and I advise you to read it as soon as possible." [22] *The Red Rover,* he remarked in his journal, displayed "much genius, a powerful conception of character, and force of execution," [23] and only two weeks later Scott had finished *The Prairie,* which he preferred to *The Red Rover.*

His opinion of *Emma*—"a story which we peruse with pleasure, if not with deep interest"—has been cited; but it did not represent his final assessment of Jane Austen. Ten years later, after reading for the third time "that very finely written novel" *Pride and Prejudice,* Scott remarked in a well-known journal entry: "That young lady had a talent for describing the involvements and feelings and characters of ordinary life, which is to me the most wonderful I ever met with. The Big Bow-wow strain I can do myself like any now going, but the exquisite touch, which renders ordinary commonplace things and characters interesting, from the truth of the description and the sentiment, is denied to me." [24]

Fundamentally, however, Scott's criticism is highly conservative in spite of the flexibility of its application. Scott's view of the nature and function of literature is thoroughly neo-classic, for his usual emphasis on the pleasure rather than the instruction provided by novels reflects his opinion of the novel as a mere diversion rather than a major literary form. In summary, the value he placed on spontaneity may seem to show a leaning toward Romanticism; but it appears to be principally a justification, perhaps unconscious, of his own method of writing. Spontaneity, to Scott, means rapid and careless composition rather than a Wordsworthian "spontaneous overflow of powerful emotion." Scott never approaches the fundamental postulate of Romantic theory—the organic concept of art.—A novel, for him, is simply the sum of its parts—plot, character, setting, style, etc.—each of which was to be considered, if it were considered, in isolation. It is now generally recognized that Scott should not be described as a Romanticist despite the superficially "romantic" settings of his works. His criticism represents the end of a tradition, a fact of which Scott shows no awareness; his is the last expression by a major writer of the neo-classic position.

CHAPTER 4

Waverley

SCOTT'S career as novelist began late (he was forty-two when *Waverley* appeared); and, according to his own account, his becoming one resulted from the chance discovery of a fragment of manuscript and from the declining popularity of his poems and the rising fame of Byron. In fact, however, Scott's whole life pointed toward the novel. From his childhood he had displayed a love of storytelling. As a boy he had been able to amuse himself and his schoolmates for hours at a time with improvised tales of chivalry; as an adult, his conversational ability lay in anecdote, for which he was famous, rather than in repartee or disputation.

Scott was always an enthusiastic novel reader, and it was natural enough that some of his first literary experiments should be in this form. Two fragments composed before 1800 have survived. The longer and more interesting, *Thomas the Rhymer*, was intended to be "a tale of chivalry . . . in the style of *The Castle of Otranto*, with plenty of Border characters and supernatural incident" [1]—a kind of prose equivalent, in fact, of *The Lay of the Last Minstrel*. *Thomas*, like its companion-piece *The Lord of Ennerdale*, never advanced beyond the opening chapter; but Scott did not lose his interest in the novel. Still another experiment, one that was published, followed—Scott's completion of Joseph Strutt's *Queenhoo Hall*. This historical novel was set in fifteenth-century England, but Strutt, a famous antiquarian, had made his book almost unreadable by its profusion of historical detail. From its failure Scott learned a useful lesson: "by rendering his language too ancient, and displaying his antiquarian knowledge too liberally, the ingenious author had raised up an obstacle to his own success. Every work designed for mere amusement must be expressed in language easily comprehended." [2] It was unnecessary and undesirable, Scott believed, to reproduce literally the language of a bygone age; it was enough to avoid obvious anachronisms, to suggest the general tone or style of the period, and perhaps to season the dialogue with an occasional archaism.

At about the same time, Scott had begun *Waverley* and completed seven chapters. The exact date of composition cannot be determined since Scott's own account, given many years later in the general preface to the Waverley Novels, is self-contradictory. "My early recollections of the Highland scenery and customs made so favourable an impression in the poem called the Lady of the Lake," Scott wrote, "that I was induced to think of attempting something of the same kind in prose. It was with some idea of this kind, that, about the year 1805, I threw together about one-third part of the first volume of Waverley." [3] But the date of 1805 is impossible since *The Lady of the Lake* was not published until 1810. What is certain is that *Waverley* was advertised in a list of forthcoming books for 1809–10. But when Scott asked the opinion of friends about the book they unanimously condemned it and *Waverley* was put aside. When Scott finally returned to it, he finished it with almost unbelievable speed, writing the last two volumes in three weeks. *Waverley, or 'Tis Sixty Years Since* was published anonymously in July, 1814.

When one considers all of these preliminary attempts, when one recognizes the steady development in his work toward longer and more complex narrative, the surprising fact is not that Scott finally became a novelist but that he waited so long to become one. The delay may be explained in part by the comparatively low prestige of the novel in his time and by the fact that verse was still considered the natural medium for narrative. (All of the major Romantic poets wrote narrative poems and so did Thomas Campbell, Thomas Moore, and George Crabbe, among others.) If Scott had been born a contemporary of Dickens rather than of Wordsworth, he probably would have turned directly to the novel and never have written poetry.

I *Critical Reception*

The year 1814 seems in retrospect a notable one in the history of English literature for it witnessed the publication not only of *Waverley* but of Wordsworth's *Excursion* (an intensely unpopular work except among a small sect of disciples) and of Jane Austen's

Mansfield Park (which enjoyed substantial but not sensational popularity); but, to contemporaries, *Waverley* overshadowed everything else. Only one reviewer, John Wilson Croker, was positively hostile. Croker pronounced dogmatically in the *Quarterly Review* that "we have a great objection . . . to historical romance, in which real and fictitious personages and actual and fabulous events are mixed together to the utter confusion of the reader and the unsettling of all accurate recollections of past transaction." [4] He wished that Scott had written a history of the Jacobite rising of 1745 instead of a novel.

More typical of critical opinion was the judgment of the *Edinburgh Review*, which found *Waverley* full of "nature and truth," so much so that its scenes and characters must have been "copied from existing originals." [5] But the public did not wait for reviewers to praise or blame. "Except for the first opening of the *Edinburgh Review*," wrote an intelligent contemporary, "no work that has appeared in my time made such an instant and universal impression. . . . The unexpected newness of the thing, the profusion of original characters, the Scotch language, Scotch scenery, Scotch men and women, the simplicity of the writing, and the graphic force of the descriptions, all struck us with an electric shock of delight . . . . If the concealment of the authorship was intended to make mystery heighten their effect, it completely succeeded. The speculations and conjectures, and nods and winks, and predictions and assertions were endless, and occupied every company, and almost every two men who met and spoke in the street." [6]

Scott might have foreseen the popularity of *Waverley* in Scotland; but he could hardly have predicted that the English audience would delight equally in Scotch scenery, characters, and even language. The English success of *Waverley* was so unprecedented that it prompted Jane Austen's humorous complaint that "Walter Scott has no business to write novels, especially good ones —It is not fair. He has fame and profit enough as a poet and should not be taking the bread out of other people's mouths. I do not mean to like *Waverley* if I can help it—but I fear I must." [7]

Many causes contributed to the popularity of the Waverley Novels—and full discussion of them is reserved for a more appropriate place—but one of them was "the unexpected newness of the thing." *Waverley* was original in its presentation of regional peculiarities—"Scotch language, Scotch scenery, Scotch men and women"—which in eighteenth-century fictions had appeared only as subjects for ridicule when they were present at all. Particularly, of course, Highland characters and "manners" were strikingly fresh and picturesque. There was little wonder that the work appealed to a public which was becoming bored with Gothic terrors. *Waverley* was new too in its use of history; in fact it can justifiably be called the first historical novel. Historical forgeries like Defoe's *Journal of the Plague Year* could hardly be considered novels; and Gothic novels, although usually vaguely medieval in setting, were completely non-historical in spirit.

The opening six chapters of the novel, however, provided a barrier high enough to test any reader's enthusiasm. Presenting Waverley's education, tastes, family history, and the political background against which he was raised, they supply essential information but are completely undramatic; they consist almost entirely of exposition that is interrupted occasionally by irrelevant intrusions of the author. Scott, who admitted their dullness, claimed he had "left the story to flag in the first volume on purpose . . . to avoid the usual error of novel writers, whose first volume is usually their best" [8]—an explanation which sounds remarkably like a rationalization. No writer as concerned with sales as Scott would have deliberately chosen to bore his readers through a whole volume. Scott, however, exaggerated by saying that the whole first volume was made dull; with Waverley's arrival at Tully-Veolan, in Chapter Eight, his true story commences.

Since *Waverley* is not among the Scott novels most widely read today, a summary of its plot ("story" might be a more accurate term) may be useful. Edward Waverley has been brought up by his rich and elderly uncle, Sir Evrard Waverley. Left much to himself, he reads widely in poetry and romance and lives in a romantic world of his own creation—a world which he associates with the past. This attitude is reinforced by the old-fashioned Toryism of his uncle and his tutor. A military career is chosen for him, and a commission is purchased in a regiment of dragoons stationed in Scotland. Bored with his duties and his associates, Waverley visits Baron Bradwardine, his uncle's old friend, at his estate of Tully-Veolan at the foot of the Highlands.

When he takes the opportunity of seeing Highland life by a visit to the clan of Mac-Ivor, he is captivated by the beauty of Flora Mac-Ivor, dominated by the fiery energy of her brother Fergus, and charmed by the picturesqueness of Highland life and the primitive loyalty of the clansmen to their chief. Meanwhile Prince Charles, the "Young Pretender" of his enemies and "bonny Prince Charlie" of his friends, has landed to reclaim the throne for the Stuart family. By force of circumstance and accident, rather than conviction, Waverley is pressed into joining the Prince's army. He falls under suspicion because of his prolonged visit to Bradwardine and Fergus, both notorious Jacobites; his return is delayed by a hunting accident; letters commanding him to return to his regiment are intercepted by the robber Donald Bean Lean, who also attempts to arouse a mutiny in Waverley's troop; finally, he is relieved of his command.

Returning to assert his innocence, Waverley is arrested by Hanoverian authorities, then rescued and held prisoner under mysterious circumstances, and finally brought to the Prince at Edinburgh. Carried away by romantic enthusiasm, by hope of winning Flora's love, by the dominating personality of Fergus, and by pressure of circumstances, he pledges himself to the prince's service and takes part in the Jacobite victory of Preston. There he rescues an English officer, Colonel Talbot. Waverley accompanies the Jacobite invasion of England, but he is separated from the army in the retreat and forced into hiding. Through the influence of Colonel Talbot, however, who has been released on parole, he gains a pardon. He witnesses the trial and condemnation to death of Fergus, marries Rose Bradwardine (after Flora more than once decisively rejects him, he decides that he loves Rose), and restores the baron's confiscated estate. Flora, grieving for her brother's death and the failure of her cause, enters a French convent. The disappearance of the letters and Waverley's mysterious imprisonment following his rescue from arrest are hastily accounted for with a naïve explanation by the author: "These circumstances will serve to explain such points of our narrative as, according to the custom of storytellers, we deemed it fit to leave unexplained, for the purpose of exciting the reader's curiosity." Everyone except the Mac-Ivors, we assume, lives happily ever after.

Such a plot is obviously "inartificial," to use Scott's own term;

and perhaps the best comment on it is provided by the author himself in his preface: "The tale of Waverley was put together with so little care, that I cannot boast of having sketched any distinct plan of the work. The whole adventures of Waverley, in his movements up and down the country with the Highland cateran Bean Lean, are managed without much skill. It suited best, however, the road I wanted to travel, and permitted me to introduce some description of scenery and manners." *Waverley* is typical in this respect; Scott habitually began writing a novel without having any idea of how it would end. Plot, to him, was primarily a means for bringing in whatever persons, events, or scenes he wished to describe. He never attempted, and was probably incapable of, a well-made plot like that of *Tom Jones*. *Waverley* approaches the picaresque form, and it perhaps would be a more successful work if Scott had not only recognized his limitation but also taken advantage of it by adhering completely to the picaresque and by abandoning the conventional baggage of a love story and a mystery.

II *Techniques*

His narrative method, as might be expected, is thoroughly conventional since Scott was simply not the kind of writer to be interested in technical experiments or in literary form for its own sake. Waverley's point of view is preserved with fair consistency, no doubt because it provides the author an opportunity to describe "manners" at length (everything seen was new to Waverley). Other characters reveal themselves primarily by speech and action, but Scott does not hesitate to offer an occasional interior view, especially to make us better acquainted with a major character at his first introduction. To the twentieth-century reader, the most disturbing formal element is the author's abundant commentary. Moreover, the modern objection to such intrusions by the author as a disastrous violation of realism was not unknown in Scott's time. The aged Henry Mackenzie, author of *The Man of Feeling*, made a thoroughly Jamesian complaint about such addresses to the reader; "you should never be forced to recollect . . . that such a work is a work of fiction, and all its fine creations but air."

Nevertheless, a dogmatic statement that all commentary is

harmful to fiction cannot be justified; too many examples prove the contrary. Its value depends upon its appropriateness and usefulness, and upon the quality of mind which it reveals. Unfortunately, when the commentary in *Waverley* is evaluated by such standards, it is often found defective. At times it is simply irrelevant and distracting, as when Scott interrupts his account of Waverley's upbringing to indulge himself with a long diatribe against modern education (a passage which sounds remarkably like a twentieth-century conservative attacking progressive education). A similar lapse occurs when, at the conclusion of Chapter Five, Scott apologizes at great length and with a rather heavy irony for plaguing his readers so long with old-fashioned politics. Or one may consider the quite unnecessary and labored whimsy which precedes the perfectly serious description of Fergus Mac-Ivor in Chapter Nineteen and undercuts its effectiveness: "It is an important examination, and therefore, like Dogberry, we must spare no wisdom."

A common judgment of Scott's contemporaries was that his characters were better than his plots, and the success of the work depended in large part on its characters—although certainly not on those of the official hero and heroine, Waverley and Rose Bradwardine. Flora Mac-Ivor strongly attracted sentimental readers who felt that Waverley should have married her (Scott's comment on this reaction was that Flora would have set him up on the mantel as the wife of Count Boralaski, a Polish dwarf, was supposed to have done with her husband). But Flora is very much a stage heroine and her language is too often the language of melodrama: "There is, Mr. Waverley, there is, a busy devil at my heart, that whispers—but it were madness to listen to it—that the strength of mind on which Flora prided herself has murdered her brother . . . it haunts me like a phantom; I know it is unsubstantial and vain; but it *will* be present; will intrude its horrors on my mind." Flora's early appearance, complete with props of harp, "shaggy copse," and "romantic waterfall," to sing a Highland war song to Waverley produces an effect of artificiality from which her characterization never really recovers.

Fergus is considerably more effective; indeed, he won the sympathies of readers from the official hero as thoroughly as Flora did from the heroine. He is the precise opposite of Waverley in every respect. Waverley is rich, Fergus comparatively poor; Waverley is passive, Fergus incessantly active; Waverley submits to circumstances or to the stronger personality, Fergus dominates; Waverley is blond, Fergus is dark. He is the "dark hero" that Scott often opposes to the passive, "official" hero. If all the conventional virtue is with the passive hero, all the life is with the dark hero. Even his language has a colloquial ease and vigor which contrast strikingly with the official hero's pompous dullness. Significantly, the dark hero always dies; Scott seems to have admired his qualities yet feared their consequences for society. The narrative poems had already created the pattern and made it so familiar that Miss Mitford recognized *Waverley* as Scott's work by, among other clues, "the hanging of the clever hero and the marrying of the stupid one." [9]

But Fergus is not merely a typical "dark hero." He is an individual of "bold, ambitious, and ardent, yet artful and politic character." A Highland chief of Jacobite sympathies in the year 1745, he is an incongruous mixture of impulse and calculation, of pride and dissimulation, of Gallic sophistication and Highland barbarism. In an admirable chapter, Scott presents Fergus' history and reveals how thoroughly he is the creature of his time and position: "Had Fergus lived Sixty Years sooner than he did, he would, in all probability, have wanted the polished manner and knowledge of the world which he now possessed; and had he lived Sixty Years later, his ambition and love of rule would have lacked the fuel which his situation now afforded." Here the author's commentary is thoroughly justified; it increases the reader's understanding of Fergus and provides the necessary information in the most efficient and economical manner. The chapter is a little historical essay, illuminating in itself and also essential to the novel.

The most complex and least "romantic" of the major characters is Baron Bradwardine. Like Fergus, he is introduced by a brief sketch of his background and summary of his character in which "the pedantry of the lawyer" is superimposed upon "the military pride of the soldier." (The Baron has had a legal education, and has served in the French armies.) He is then allowed to reveal himself in his welcoming monologue to Waverley as a litigious, impoverished, rank-conscious gentleman who is proud of his Latin tags and French phrases. His pride is enormous yet inoffensive, perhaps because so unconscious, as demonstrated by his comment on the Laird of Killancureit, whose father had been a steward: "And God forbid, Captain Waverley, that we of irreproachable lineage should exult over him, when it may be, that in the eighth, ninth, or tenth generation, his progeny may rank, in a manner, with the old gentry of the country." The irony of this mock-humility is excellent in itself and still more so in its innocent self-revelation, which reveals more subtlety than Scott is usually credited with.

The baron's pride in his rank and family, his despotic authority over his tenants, and his devoted Jacobitism closely resemble Fergus Mac-Ivor's characteristics; but Scott carefully discriminates between the two characters. The baron's power, limited to one wretched village, seems a ridiculous anachronism. He is absurd in success (as in his insistence on his hereditary privilege of removing the royal boots of his sovereign after a battle), but he is dignified and even heroic in defeat. His culture is solidly founded on classical literature, and his allusions remind us of a broader world than Scotland and of the essential continuity of the human condition. He is a pedant, yet capable of translating the Latin poets into a vigorous vernacular. The character is not a mere "humour," as similar characters often became in Scott's later works, but one which displays new facets and changes and grows throughout the novel.

Scott's own favorite character, though he did not expect his choice to be anyone else's, was Bailie MacWheeble. Cautious (if not cowardly), selfish, calculating, sly, and self-serving, yet devoted to his master's interests (next to his own), he is a type that Scott loved to portray. The Bailie's combination of subservience toward superiors and of arrogance toward inferiors is revealed even in his posture; at the table

to preserve that proper declination of person which showed a sense that he was in the presence of his patron, he sat upon the edge of his chair, placed at three feet distance from the table . . . projecting his person towards it in a line which obliqued from the bottom of his spine. . . . This stooping position might have been inconvenient to another person; but long habit made it, whether seated or walking, perfectly easy to the worthy Bailie. In the latter posture, it occasioned, no doubt, an unseemly projection of the person towards those who happened to walk behind; but those being at all times his inferiors . . . he cared very little what inference of contempt or slight regard they might derive from the circumstance.

Whenever a lower-class character appears, speaking his native Scots, the person comes instantly and memorably to life, no matter how brief his appearance. One should note, for example, the Jacobite wife of the village smith whom Waverley encounters in the village of Cairnvreckan. A "strong, large-boned, hard-featured woman, about forty, dressed as if her clothes had been flung on with a pitchfork" is speaking to the villagers: "And that's a' your Whiggery, and your presbytery, ye cut-lugged, graning carles! What! d'ye think the lads wi' the kilts will care for yer synods and yer presbyteries, and yer buttock-mail, and yer stool o' repentance?" Equally good is the plea of the elders of the village: "Whisht, gudewife; is this a time; or is this a day, to be singing your ranting fule sangs in?—a time when the wine of wrath is poured out without mixture in the cup of indignation, and a day when the land should give testimony against popery, and prelacy, and quakerism, and independency, and supremacy, and erastianism, and antinomianism, and a' the errors of the church?" Scott's presentation is completely without sentimentality—one of its main strengths. Presbyterian fanatic, village shrew, or drunken horse trader, Scott presents them objectively; and he allows them, unlike his aristocrats, to speak their natural language.

III *Language*

Primarily, the effectiveness of characterization in *Waverley* depends upon the language which the characters speak; the more strongly Scottish the speech, the more vigorous and individual the character. At one extreme are the peasants and burghers speaking their broad Scots; at the other are the hero and heroine, conversing in standard English. But the term "standard English" is misleading; no language resembling it could ever have been spoken. It is trite, redundant, Latinate, involved; often absurd, it is disastrous when intense feeling is to be expressed. Out of a hundred possible examples, one may consider the dialogue in which Flora rejects Waverley's suit, and he asks her reasons:

"Forgive me, Mr. Waverley," said Flora . . . "I should incur my own heavy censure, did I delay expressing my sincere conviction that I can never regard you otherwise than as a valued friend . . . oh, better a thousand times, Mr. Waverley, that you should feel a present momentary disappointment, than the long and heart-sickening griefs which attend a rash and ill-assorted marriage!"

"Good God!" exclaimed Waverley, "why should you anticipate such consequences from a union, where birth is equal, where fortune is favourable, where, if I may venture to say so, the tastes are similar, where you allege no preference for another, where you even express a favourable opinion of him whom you reject?"

Hardly the language of passion! One notes the hackneyed remark that Waverley can only be a friend; the elaborate parallelism of Waverley's reply—"where birth," "where fortune," "where the tastes," "where you allege," "where you even"—carried on through five subordinate clauses; the redundancy of Flora—"*heavy* censure," "*sincere* conviction," "present *momentary* disappointment," "rash and ill-assorted marriage"; the careful inversion "did I delay,"; and the elaborate propriety—comic at such a moment—of Waverley's "if I may venture to say so." Waverley's surprise and bitter disappointment simply are not communicated. We have Scott's word that Waverley feels strongly; but the author's word is not enough—and here it is directly contradicted by the language of the hero. Strong personal feeling cannot be expressed in such a style.

In another example, Colonel Talbot, whom Waverley rescues at the Battle of Preston, is described as a blunt, practical soldier; but this is how he talks at a moment of emotion: "It is a responsibility, Heaven knows, sufficiently heavy for mortality, that we must answer for the foreseen and direct result of our actions,—for their indirect and consequential operation, the great and good Being, who alone can foresee the dependence of human events on each other, hath not pronounced his frail creatures liable." Again, the character's speech destroys the impression that the author plainly intended to create.

Scott is frequently no more successful with direct description of his characters than with their dialogue, and again the fault is primarily of language. As an example, there is the description of Fergus Mac-Ivor in a rage: "The veins of his forehead swelled when he was in such agitation; his nostril became dilated; his cheek and eye inflamed; and his look became that of a demoniac. These appearances of half-suppressed rage were the more frightful, because they were obviously caused by a strong effort to temper with discretion an almost ungovernable paroxysm of passion, and resulted from an internal conflict of the most dreadful kind, which agitated his whole frame of mortality." In the first sentence one notices the triteness of the symptoms and their melodramatic exaggeration; in the second, the abstractness of the language and its extreme redundancy—"whole frame of mortality" for "body." Certainly any excitement aroused by the preceding sentence is effectively damped. The whole speech is a deplorable combination of melodrama and vagueness.

Vagueness of language is of course both a cause and a consequence of vagueness of conception, as the following passage suggests: "Rose Bradwardine rose gradually in Waverley's opinion. He had several opportunities of remarking, that, as her extreme timidity wore off, her manners assumed a higher character; that the agitating circumstances of the stormy time seemed to call forth a certain dignity of feeling and expression which he had not formerly observed; and that she omitted no opportunity within her reach to extend her knowledge and refine her taste." It is hard to imagine what Scott could have had in mind in the phrases about extending knowledge and refining taste. Did Rose study geometry, perhaps? Or practice the harpsichord? It seems probable that the author himself didn't know what he meant and was not sufficiently interested to take the trouble of giving content to his language. As for the "dignity of feeling and expression" and the "higher character" of her manners, such generalities are useless without illustration by action or speech.

This charge of vagueness applies even more seriously to the presentation of Waverley, who is much more important in the novel than Rose. Scott repeatedly tries to make his hero more interesting and "romantic" and consistently fails because his efforts are limited to general description. A good example occurs in Chapter Forty-three, which describes the ball held by the Jacobites in Holyrood Castle just before the Battle of Preston: "Waverley exerted his powers of fancy, animation, and eloquence, and attracted the general admiration of the company. . . . Waverley, as we have elsewhere observed, possessed at times a wonderful flow of rhetoric; and . . . touched more than once the higher notes of feeling, and then again ran off in a wild voluntary of fanciful mirth." Finally, the Prince observes "He is really one of the most fascinating young men whom I have ever seen." But Waverley has never shown us these powers with which he is suddenly credited; and, since he has never displayed his wonderful flow of rhetoric, the reader cannot possibly imagine its nature. One must assume either that Scott himself had only the vaguest notion of the meaning of "higher notes of feeling" or "wild voluntary of fanciful mirth," or that to present them was beyond his ability. At the end of the scene Scott tells us that Flora Mac-Ivor changed her previous opinion that Waverley's manners indicated "timidity and imbecility of disposition." But the reader has formed a similar judgment and is given no reason to change it.

Passages like these justify Edwin Muir's observation that Scott's prose is "a unique combination of bookishness and slovenliness . . . no matter what he has to say, Scott seems resolved to say it in the dullest way possible, and in the slowest." [10] This debased Johnsonese is, after all, the principal medium of Scott's narrative. One's objection is not merely that it is undistinguished, but that it impedes the movement of the story, blurs and generalizes the scenes and actions described, frequently contradicts the author's intended effect, and makes impossible the expression of any kind of genuine feeling.

IV   *Dramatic Presentation*

Although Scott was often praised by his contemporaries for the dramatic quality of his dialogue, he failed to realize the importance of the scene and as a result frequently misses his opportunities. The ball offered the occasion for a brilliant scene which would have served a useful function by displaying new facets of Waverley's character, but Scott chose to rely on narration and description rather than to make the effort of dramatization. The result is complete dullness. An even more striking failure follows in the account, or rather non-account, of the Battle of Preston. The Highlanders charge, Waverley among them; and Scott dryly remarks that "The rest is well known" and then summarizes the outcome in a short paragraph. It might be argued that Scott was not writing a history of the rebellion and was not bound to describe every episode. But here some ten thousand words of continuous narrative—the ball at Holyrood, a detailed description of the rebel army on the march, the maneuvers of the opposing forces, the camp of the Highlanders, and their march through darkness and fog to reach the battle field, the sudden clearing of the mist and sight of the Hanoverian army—have prepared the reader for a climax which never comes.

On occasion, certainly, Scott can create an effective and revealing scene. Perhaps the most powerfully moving passage in *Waverly* is Fergus' trial and condemnation. Scott's narrative is clear and concise; his language, understated. The touch of staginess in Fergus' speech to the judge is immediately offset by the simplicity and unconscious humor of Evan's appeal for the life of his chief: "let him gae back to France, and no to trouble King George's government again, that only six o' the very best of his clan will be willing to be justified in his stead; and if you'll just let me gae down to Glennaquoich, I'll fetch them up to ye mysell, to head or hang, and you may begin wi' me. . . ." This speech is followed by the plainness and dignity of his reproof to the laughing spectators: "if they laugh because they think I would not keep my word, and come back to redeem him, I can tell them they ken neither the heart of a Hielandman, nor the honor of gentlemen." Evan speaks in the vernacular; Scott never achieved such a quality with standard English.

An even more striking effect is obtained, again with the vernacular, when the reader's emotions have been worked upon to the highest degree by Waverley's final conversation with Fergus in his cell and by the appeal to his sympathy of the savage punishment (he is to be hanged, drawn, and quartered) which is imminent. As Waverley leaves Carlisle, his servant sums up the matter: "It's a great pity of Evan Dhu, who was a very weel-meaning, good-natured man, to be a Hielandman; and indeed so was the Laird of Glennaquoich too, for that matter, when he wasna in ane o' his tirrivies." Suddenly Scott has brought the reader from the tragic plane to a level on which he can be expected to take an interest in the winding up of the plot and Waverley's marriage to Rose.

Equally successful is the drinking-bout with which Baron Bradwardine welcomes Waverley. There is no attempt to make narrative do the work of dialogue; the baron and his cronies (particularly the oafish Balmawhapple) reveal themselves in their natural speech. The increasing befuddlement, as first the Blessed Bear of Bradwardine (the baron's huge ceremonial goblet) and then the Tappit Hen (the village landlady's pot) circulate, is shown by the growing confusion, the mutual interruptions, the insults and anger which culminate in the inevitable brawl as Bradwardine and Balmawhapple draw their swords on each other. The whole scene is a first-rate piece of comedy, and a brilliant satirical presentation of "manners." A companion-piece follows a few chapters later with the account of Fergus' feast for his clan. In it Scott creates a patriarchal society, with more obvious resemblance to Homeric Greece than to eighteenth-century England. The scene constitutes Scott's most extended portrayal of Highland manners.

V *Thematic Unity*

Scott's contemporaries were apparently content to delight in the exciting action, the striking characters, the picturesque scenery, and the faithful accounts of "manners" without looking for further significance. Most critics today demand more of a novel if it is to be considered as a work of art, and so it is not surprising that critics intent on "saving" *Waverley* have attempted to give it thematic unity, even if unity of structure seems to be lacking. S. Stewart Gordon has suggested that the central significance of the novel lies in the conflict between Waverley's sound and unsound judgment or, in different terms, between romance and reality. The conflict, for Gordon, provides the fundamental unity of the novel; and much evidence can be found to support his interpretation. Waverley's early reading disgusts him with the actual world of busy, practical England; and in Scotland he seems to discover the past of his imagination. On hearing of the raid on the baron's cattle and Rose's account of past troubles with the Highlanders, "Waverley could not help starting at a story which bore so much resemblance to one of his own day-dreams. Here was a girl . . . who had witnessed with her own eyes such a scene as he had used to conjure up in his imagination, as only occurring in ancient times. He might have said to himself . . . 'I am actually in the land of military and romantic adventures, and it only remains to

be seen what will be my own share in them.'" Traveling toward
the cave of the robber Bean Lean, Waverley intensely enjoys himself: "Here he sat on the banks of an unknown lake, under the
guidance of a wild native, whose language was unknown to him,
on a visit to the den of some renowned outlaw, a second Robin
Hood, perhaps . . . and that at deep midnight, through scenes of
difficulty and toil. . . . What a variety of incidents for the exercise of his romantic imagination . . . . The only circumstance
which assorted ill with the rest, was the cause of his journey—the
Baron's milk cows! this degrading incident he kept in the background."

The robber's cave is so intensely picturesque that Waverley
"prepared himself to meet a stern, gigantic, ferocious figure, such
as Salvator would have chosen to be the central object of a group
of banditti." Disillusionment quickly follows, when Donald Bean
Lean turns out to be "diminutive and insignificant" and is dressed
in a cast-off uniform; but Waverley fails to profit by the lesson
and to realize that there is nothing in the least romantic about
Donald or his exploits. Naturally, Waverley is carried away with
enthusiasm when he takes part in the feast of the clan of Ivor. If
Tully-Veolan and Baron Bradwardine had seemed to return him
to the feudal age, this tribal society, with its aged bard chanting a
war song, belongs to a still earlier period of history. Waverley, the
outsider, is swept away by the romance of the occasion, but Fergus, the chief, is immune—"The Chieftain . . . during this scene
[the bard's song], had appeared rather to watch the emotions
which were excited, than to partake of their high tone of enthusiasm." Waverley's enthusiasm for the Highlanders is simply the
result of delight in their picturesque costumes and customs. Its
quality is suggested by the "large and spirited painting," which he
orders later, "representing Fergus Mac-Ivor and Waverley in their
Highland dress, the scene a wild, rocky, and mountainous pass,
down which the clan were descending in the background."

Waverley, then, is prepared for such a "military and romantic
adventure" as the Jacobite rising; and any remaining judgment is
overcome by the glamor of Prince Charles, who seems to him a
"hero of romance." He quickly forgets his rational view, that
whatever the legal claims of the Stuarts to the throne might be, it
was hardly worthwhile "to disturb a government so long settled

and established, and to plunge a kingdom into all the miseries of civil war, for the purpose of replacing upon the throne the descendants of a monarch by whom it had been wilfully forfeited." Disenchantment soon begins, however, when Waverley witnesses the reality of civil war at Preston; and it is increased by the arguments of his prisoner, Colonel Talbot, who is entirely immune to the claims of sentiment and romance, and by the absence of popular enthusiasm as the rebels march into England.

Waverley finally has enough of the glory of war: "The plumed troops and the big war used to enchant me in poetry; but the night marches, vigils, couches under the wintry sky, and such accompaniments of the glorious trade, are not at all to my taste in practice.' Cut off from the prince's army, and without hope of rejoining it, he "felt himself entitled to say firmly, though perhaps with a sigh, that the romance of his life was ended, and that its real history had now commenced." Scott indeed appears to have intended to present in Waverley "that . . . aberration from sound judgment which apprehends occurrences in their reality, but communicates to them a tincture of its own romantic tone and colouring." The danger of such "tincturing," Waverley's career abundantly illustrates.

To Waverley at the outset, England represented reality; Scotland, romance. This contrast is repeated in a series of oppositions: Lowland-Highland, Hanoverian-Jacobite, Rose Bradwardine and Flora Mac-Ivor, Colonel Talbot and Fergus, a shrewd and ambitious politician, who seems to Waverley "the incarnation of romance." As Waverley returns to England with the prince's army, realism sets in quickly; and he is relieved when circumstances separate him from the Jacobite army and allow him an honorable escape from a lost cause. By the conclusion of the novel he is quite content to marry Rose, who will make a much more comfortable wife than Flora. The romance of life is dismissed, "perhaps with a sigh"—Waverley is careful to preserve his weapons and Highland dress as souvenirs—but nevertheless firmly.

This theme is undoubtedly carried through the work with a good deal of consistency, but it is a less important part of the total effect than it should be. The trouble is that the reader is not interested enough in Waverley himself, who embodies and illustrates the contrast. Waverley's conversion from romance to reality requires a psychological change which Scott does not represent; he simply states from time to time that a change is taking place, and at last that it is concluded. Scott assures the reader that Waverley finally "acquired a more complete mastery of a spirit tamed by adversity, than his former experience had given him"; but, as is usually the case with statements about Waverley, the assertion does not convince because it is not demonstrated. The "happy ending" is not made possible by any change in the hero but by his lucky inheritance of a fortune and by the influence of his friends. What the reader sees, as distinguished from what the author may have intended, is not a hero gradually maturing through the lessons of experience but rather, in the words of a contemporary critic, a character "ineffectually repenting, snatched away by accident from his sinking party: by accident preserved from justice; and restored by the exertions of his friends to safety, fortune, and happiness." [11]

VI *As Historical Novel*

One most important aspect remains to be considered: *Waverley* as a historical novel. A vaguely medieval setting was no novelty in early nineteenth-century fiction, but the remark of Georg Lukacs that Scott was the first novelist to reveal the "derivation of the individuality of characters from the historical peculiarities of their age" appears justified. As has been noted, Fergus is carefully and precisely placed historically, and this placement is as effective, although less explicit, for Bradwardine, Colonel Talbot, Evan Dhu Maccombich, Donald Bean Lean, and even Bailie MacWheeble. The historical setting, solid and accurate, is delineated without pedantry or excessive detail. Scott had read the available sources, but his most important knowledge had been gained firsthand from survivors of the rebellion. His own ancestors had fought for the Stuarts in 1690 and 1715; as a child he had listened to the stories of survivors of the '45 and had become "a valiant Jacobite at the age of ten." [12] These events were not part of a remote and alien past; they formed a central part of the recent history of his country. His relationship to them is similar to that of Tolstoy to the Napoleonic invasion of Russia. It seems possible that "sixty years since" is almost the limit to which a novelist's imagination can penetrate; a novel dealing with the more distant past tends to become an archaeological reconstruction, tempered by anachronisms.

The reader's emotions, like Waverley's, inevitably go with the Jacobites, even though common sense may reluctantly prefer George II. Certainly Scott's treatment does justice, perhaps a little more than justice, to the rising as a chivalrous adventure. Yet intelligence does not abdicate; it is present in the arguments of Colonel Talbot, and in Waverley's second thoughts as he sees the reality of civil war. An anachronism in comfortable, rational mid-eighteenth-century Great Britain, the rising is an effort to restore the past, one of "romance" and "honor" perhaps, but also of poverty (strongly emphasized in Scott's description of the village of Tully-Veolan), bloodshed, and disorder. The point is made explicit by Evan Dhu, Fergus' second-in-command, when he taunts Bailie MacWheeble: "The gude auld times of rugging and riving (pulling and tearing) are come back again" and the law must give way to the longest sword. It is significant, incidentally, that Gifted Gilfillan and his troop of irregulars, who so strikingly resemble the Roundheads and Covenanters of the previous century, are ignominiously routed by the Highlanders. The rebellion is not to be defeated by another anachronism.

One may learn a great deal of history from *Waverley* (*pace* Richards and all modern critics who insist that literature can make only pseudo-statements), yet it is clearly absurd to insist, as the *Quarterly Review* did, that the interest and value of the work derive "not from any of the ordinary qualities of a novel, but from the truth of its facts, and the accuracy of its delineations." [13] Without the "ordinary [or perhaps extraordinary] qualities" of a novel, *Waverley* would be valueless.

Scott does not give, and clearly did not intend to give, a full picture of the rising. The novel omits the landing of the prince in the Highlands, accompanied by only seven followers, and the final defeat at Culloden—both striking events and ones essential to a complete account. Scott was not writing history but a novel, and his subject was not so much the rebellion itself as the "manners" which it allowed him to display—particularly the contrast between past and present, the past being represented by Scotland (especially the Highlands) and the Jacobites, the present by England and the Hanoverians. In spite of the glamour of the past, which Scott fully realizes and presents, its defeat is shown to be beneficial, or at any rate necessary. Yet the pathos of its defeat and disappearance is inescapable (the reader should be aware of the destruction of Lowland feudalism and Highland clanship which followed the rebellion). We find in *Waverley* a conflict and a theme which recurs often in Scott's work, and which provide the underlying unity and seriousness that make *Waverley* a frequently moving and impressive work in spite of its glaring faults of construction and style.

VII Redgauntlet

Ten years after the publication of *Waverley*, Scott presented in *Redgauntlet* (1824) the final phase of the Jacobite movement. "*Redgauntlet* and *Waverley*," a recent critic has remarked, "are Scott's most successful attempts to define his feelings towards the Old Scotland and the New." [14] During the twenty years after 1745, Jacobitism had entered its final decline; and it would soon be no more than a sentimental or antiquarian affectation, less significant than the displays of Confederate flags in twentieth-century America. The Highlands had been reduced to order for the first time in history, Scotland had prospered as it never had before, and it had also produced a brilliant intellectual life. Under such conditions, Jacobitism must have appeared irrelevant. Nevertheless, hope died slowly among the faithful of the Jacobite movement, and historians record a steady succession of plots, always unsuccessful and usually betrayed to the government. One of these even brought Charles Edward, the Pretender, to England. Hugh Redgauntlet's plot, and the accompanying return of Charles, are purely fictitious events; but they described what very easily *could* have been.

No other Scott novel is dominated so completely by one character. If the book contrasts the old Scotland and the new, the old is summed up in Redgauntlet. His first appearance is most revealing; he is engaged in salmon-spearing from horseback and, of course, excels everyone else. The sport—picturesque, adventurous, and archaic—is typical of the man; and the central contrast of the novel is symbolized by the contrast between Redgauntlet's fish-spearing and the vastly more efficient fish-traps of the Quaker Joshua Geddes. Redgauntlet's formal dress, too, is symbolic of his personality; it "was not in the present taste, and though it had once been magnificent, was now antiquated and unfashionable." His physical strength and his skill in sports and with weapons are great, and his personal force is such that he intimidates everyone he meets. His determination, energy, and intelligence have enabled him, single-handed, to hold the Jacobite movement together, and to persuade its reluctant leaders to act, or at any rate promise to act, once more.

But his weaknesses are as obvious as his strength. Violence always seems possible when he is present, for his temper is savage and scarcely under control. A more serious weakness still is his inability to recognize, or admit, reality. He simply refuses to acknowledge the changes which have taken place during twenty years. Thus, he kidnaps his nephew, Darsie, because of Darsie's supposed authority over the tenants of the former Redgauntlet estates (which were confiscated after the 1745). But the effort is useless; even if Darsie gave the order to rise in rebellion (which he has no intention of doing), no one would follow him because the feudal allegiance of tenant to landlord had been annulled. A conversation between Darsie and his sister Lilias reveals the reality:

"Whatever these people may pretend to evade your uncle's importunities, they cannot, at this time of day, think of subjecting their necks again to the feudal yoke, which was effectually broken by the Act of 1748, abolishing vassalage and hereditary jurisdiction."

"Ay, but that my uncle considers as the act of a usurping government," said Lilias.

"Like enough *he* may think so," answered her brother, "for he is a superior, and loses his authority by the enactment. But the question is what the vassals will think of it, who have gained their freedom from feudal slavery, and have now enjoyed that freedom for many years?"

Throughout the novel there is this sense of a changing time. Much of the action takes place by the Solway River, on the border between Scotland and England; and John Buchan has commented justly that "In the book we have the sense of being always on a borderland—not only between two different races, but between comfort and savagery and between an old era and a new." [15] Redgauntlet's qualities are no longer the most valuable. Old Saunders

Fairford, lawyer and good Whig, may have fled rather ingloriously at the Battle of Falkirk, during the rebellion; but his son defends him: "He has courage enough to do what is right, and to spurn what is wrong—courage enough to defend a righteous cause with hand and purse, and to take the part of the poor man against his oppressor, without fear of the consequences to himself. This is civil courage . . . and it is of little consequence to most men in this age and country whether they ever possess military courage or no." Courage of this kind is less showy than Redgauntlet's, but it is more useful to society. Scotland had become a society of law, in which arms were needed only by soldiers and the police.

The most notable among the lesser characters of *Redgauntlet* is Peter Peebles, who, like a figure from Dickens, has been reduced to beggary and near-madness by an endless, infinitely complicated lawsuit. Peebles' absorption in a suit which has ruined his life (perhaps significantly, it began in 1745, the year of the rebellion) parallels Redgauntlet's devotion to his cause. In fact, Peebles is as pure a fanatic for the law as Redgauntlet is for the Pretender. For a moment he becomes considerably more than comic relief when he remarks of an old woman whom he had once prosecuted for debt: "She might live or die, for what I care. . . . What business have folk to do to live that canna live as the law will, and satisfy their just and lawful creditors?" Both Peebles and Redgauntlet are fanatics in their cause; both sacrifice their lives; both refuse to acknowledge a hostile reality. Scott himself enforces the parallel when Peebles exclaims: "A great year it was; the Grand Rebellion broke out, and my cause—the great cause—Peebles against Plainstanes . . . was called in the beginning of the winter session." The very suggestion of such a parallel of course indicates that Redgauntlet's heroics are not to be taken with complete seriousness.

Redgauntlet's actual plot is desperate; he plans to raise five hundred men, seize the town of Carlisle (where Jacobites had been executed after the rising of 1745), and proclaim Charles king. Then Redgauntlet will wait for the Highland regiments to defect, for disbanded soldiers to join the cause, and for the English Jacobite landlords to raise their supporters. He exaggerates every appearance of discontent and takes them as signs of readi-

ness for revolution. Like Melville's Ahab, Redgauntlet is a mono-
maniac who uses rational means for the pursuit of an irrational
and unattainable purpose. That the plot is hollow, the reader is
never allowed to doubt. "You'll as soon raise the dead as raise the
Highlands; you'll as soon get a grunt from a dead sow as any
comfort from Wales or Cheshire," remarks the realistic Nanty
Ewart, who explains Redgauntlet's apparent success: "He gets en-
couragement from some, because they want a spell of money from
him; and from others, because they fought for the cause once, and
are ashamed to go back; and others, because they have nothing to
lose; and others, because they are discontented fools."

The final scene, in which the "bubble," as the plot is often referred to, explodes, is the most complex and significant of the
novel. It has been thoroughly prepared for, and the reader's curiosity has been most successfully aroused (not through curiosity
about what will happen, for he is sure the plot will fail, but
through curiosity as to how much substance Redgauntlet's con-
spiracy actually has, and how he will react to failure). The Jacobite leaders have gathered, at Redgauntlet's urging, for what he
considers the prelude to instant rebellion, but for what they think
is merely a consultation. The meeting itself shows the hopelessness
of the cause, in the reluctance of the conspirators and in their
growing dismay as Redgauntlet removes one by one their pretexts
for delay, particularly when they learn that Charles is actually
there, ready to lead them. Then Charles defeats his own cause (as
so many of his ancestors had also done) by his stubbornness; he
refuses to accept the conspirators' condition that he abandon his
mistress, who is suspected of treachery.

To insure the defeat of the plotters who are already divided and
about to withdraw, government troops arrive (the whole scheme
has been betrayed by Redgauntlet's servant); and the Jacobites
suddenly rally and determine at least to die heroically in defense
of their prince. A dramatic moment ensues when Charles refuses
to flee: "Many threw themselves at his feet with weeping and en-
treaty; some one or two slunk in confusion from the apartment,
and were heard riding off." The entrance at this moment of General Campbell, the government commander, is a triumph of un-
derstatement: "Amid this scene of confusion, a gentleman, plainly
dressed in a riding-habit, with a black cockade [the Hanoverian

emblem] in his hat, but without any arms except a *couteau-de-chasse*, walked into the apartment without ceremony." Beside the Jacobites, he seems an incarnation of common sense and practicality. Campbell's announcement is surprising but logical: the plotters are asked only to return home quietly and everything will be forgotten, while Charles is free to embark for the Continent. Officially, the general declines to recognize the Pretender's existence. "The cause is lost forever!" exclaims Redgauntlet; and he is right. No one but himself will accompany Charles.

So Jacobitism is not allowed a final flourish of heroism and martyrdom; it is simply dismissed as something that no longer matters. Scott's theme, David Daiches has remarked, is the absurdity or irrelevance of heroic action; and the entire novel has created a world in which there is no place for a Redgauntlet or for the Jacobite cause. Andrew Lang considers it a defect in the novel that "Redgauntlet is exaggerated . . . and his wild schemes are scarcely sane," but the fact that his schemes are scarcely sane is precisely the point. Redgauntlet undoubtedly seems "exaggerated" at times, with "his stately bearing, his fatal frown, his eye of threat and of command." Daiches attributes this quality to Scott's conscious design, referring to his "melodramatic posturings (which are not defects in the novel; Scott introduces them deliberately)" and he adds that these posturings "reveal the essential unreality of the world he lives in." [16] The point, however, seems to be not that Redgauntlet is a *poseur*—his heroism is perfectly genuine—but that even genuine heroism, in such a cause, cannot help seeming slightly absurd. The theme, Daiches continues, "is a modification of that of Cervantes, and, specifically, *Redgauntlet* is Scott's *Don Quixote*." [17] This comment is acceptable if one does not try to press the parallel too far, and if one remembers that *Redgauntlet* is not the only novel in which Scott deals with such a theme.

CHAPTER 5

Guy Mannering *and* The Antiquary

THE year 1814 was an amazingly productive one, even for Scott. After writing most of *Waverley, The Lord of the Isles,* and the *Life of Swift,* in the final six weeks he tossed off *Guy Mannering,* a three-volume novel. In spite of the success of *Waverley,* he made one more attempt at the long poem with *The Lord of the Isles,* dealing with the career of Robert the Bruce and describing the Battle of Bannockburn; but by Scott's standard—sales —the poem was a comparative failure. Scott received the disappointing news like a good businessman; he simply remarked that, since one line had failed, he must try another.

When *Guy Mannering* was published four months later, in May, 1815, its success was immediate and reaffirmed the popularity of the "new Line" begun with *Waverley.* Scott had become primarily a novelist and remained one for the rest of his career in spite of many distractions. Rather surprisingly, no other Waverley novel appeared in 1815. The remainder of the year was occupied with excursions to London (where Scott met Byron), Paris, and Flanders, and these visits were followed by the composition of a thoroughly bad poem, "The Field of Waterloo," which enjoyed a considerable success because of its timeliness, and a short prose account of his European journey. Late in the year Scott returned to fiction with *The Antiquary,* which was published in the spring of 1816 and enjoyed the success of its predecessors.

I Guy Mannering

The qualities in *Guy Mannering* that so delighted Scott's contemporaries are presented by Lockhart in a comprehensive statement: "The easy transparent flow of its style; the . . . wild, solemn magnificence of its sketches of scenery; the rapid . . . interest of the narrative, the unaffected kindliness of feeling, the manly purity of thought, everywhere mingled with a gentle humour and a homely sagacity, but, above all, the rich variety and skillful contrast of characters and manners, at once fresh in fiction, and stamped with the unforgettable seal of truth and nature; these were charms that spoke to every heart and mind." [1]

Lockhart praises the "rapid interest" of the narrative, but not its construction, which would hardly admit of praise. Scott had begun writing one novel, then decided to write another, but had failed to revise his opening accordingly. His first intention had been to base his story on a legend of an astrologer whose prediction of great danger for the hero on his twenty-first birthday is fulfilled. He had intended, he explains in the introduction, to make his story "out of the incidents of the life of a doomed individual, whose efforts at good and virtuous conduct were to be forever disappointed by the intervention, as it were, of some malevolent being, and who was at last to come off victorious from the fearful struggle. The scheme projected may be traced in the three or four first chapters of the work, but further consideration induced the author to lay his purpose aside." Scott then explains how "in changing his plans . . . which was done in the course of printing, the early sheets retained the vestiges of the original tenor of the story, although they now hang upon it as an unnecessary and unnatural encumbrance." In order to speed publication, Scott was in the habit of sending each chapter to the printer as soon as it was completed, a method which of course would not permit revision in case of a change of plan. So Guy Mannering's astrological forecast remained, although it has no real function and is quite inconsistent with Mannering's character as it later developed.

In place of his original scheme, Scott developed a narrative of a missing heir. Harry Bertram, last male descendant of a decaying Scottish family, the Bertrams of Ellangowan, is kidnapped in early childhood by the smuggler Dirk Hatteraick. As a young man, ignorant of his true identity, he accidentally returns to his native region. The Bertram estate has somehow been usurped by the lawyer Glossin, who recognizes young Bertram (or Brown, as he is called at this stage) and, with the aid of Hatteraick, tries in various ways to dispose of him. Brown, who survives their machinations, is finally restored to his name, his estate, and his place in society. The novel takes its name from the English Colonel Mannering, a retired soldier who settles in the area and whose daughter Brown-Bertram finally marries.

If anything, *Guy Mannering* shows a regression in technique from *Waverley*. The Fieldingesque commentary is dropped, but Scott recurs at times to the still earlier epistolary technique of Richardson, a device which he handles most awkwardly, as when Colonel Mannering, on returning to Scotland after seventeen years, immediately sits down to write to a friend in order to tell him everything that has happened in the past seventeen years. Scott quotes from Sheridan's burlesque, *The Critic*, for one of his chapter epigraphs, and this letter strongly reminds one of an earlier passage in that play, when Mr. Puff defends his tragedy against Sneer's remark that there is no reason that one character should be so communicative as to relate to the audience, on his first appearance, all of the historical and dramatic background which they need to follow the action. "Egad," answers Puff, "that is one of the most ungrateful observations I ever heard—for the less inducement he has to tell all this, the more I think you ought to be oblig'd to him; for I am sure you'd know nothing of the matter without it." Certainly without this letter we would know nothing of Mannering's duel in India with the hero, Vanbeest Brown.

Andrew Lang, in his introduction to *Guy Mannering* in the Border Edition of the Waverley Novels, advises the reader not to analyze but to read; and, if one does so, he finds obvious attractions. In place of the Highlanders and Jacobites of *Waverley*, there are gypsies and smugglers, a pair of heroes (three, if Mannering is included) with matching heroines, and a brace of sharply contrasted villains. There are Meg Merrilies, the ancient gypsy wise woman; and Dandie Dinmont, the farmer; and especially Dandie's dogs. The episodes include a jail-break, an attack by smugglers on a country house, a combat with robbers, a presentation of gypsy burial customs, a kidnapping, and a mysterious murder; there is high life and low life. There is even a touch of the detective story in the account of the sheriff's investigation of the murder of Frank Kennedy, the gauger (customs official), and the conviction of Dirk Hatteraick seventeen years later because his foot matched the measurements taken of footprints at the scene of the crime. There is, as Lockhart pointed out, much picturesque scenery, described at length.

Above all, readers of the era enjoyed the characters. Dinmont, Meg, and Hatteraick were compared, for originality and truth, to the creations of Shakespeare (the comparison with Shakespeare was already standard with Scott's admirers). Perhaps the most admired was Meg Merrilies, who, with her six-foot height and her red cloak, unquestionably makes a striking figure. She is clearly intended as a kind of embodiment of Fate, a point made quite explicitly and emphasized by her language: "Tell him the time's coming now, and the weird's dreed, and the wheel's turning." Unfortunately, Scott alternately exaggerates and treats her with excessive caution. This touch of the theatrical about Meg is partly but by no means entirely the result of her deliberate assumption of a role. Her language frequently seems forced and "literary," as in the example above. The verb "dree," according to the Oxford English Dictionary, was revived as an archaism by Scott after having disappeared from use for three hundred years. Her curse on Godfrey Bertram, with its refrain "Ride your ways, Laird of Ellangowan," represents a striking extension of the possibilities of the vernacular; but the effect is reduced by Meg's pose high on a bank as she speaks, since the incident compels recollection of Gray's Bard. Her song, "Twist ye, twine ye! even so/Mingle shades of joy and woe," with its odd mixture of neo-classic and sentimental diction—"While the mystic twist is spinning/And the infant's life beginning"—is, as Coleridge noted, quite incongruous with the character and is as well extremely bad verse. But, while Meg is frequently melodramatized, so to speak, Scott's rationalism apparently prevented him from presenting her with complete seriousness in her own terms. Instead, he occasionally feels the need to assure his enlightened audience that *he*, of course, is not taken in by his character. After Meg has made an impressive appearance before Charles Hazlewood, the second hero, Scott proceeds to explain at length, and to undercut his own scene: "It would seem that the appearance of this female, and the mixture of frenzy and enthusiasm in her manner, seldom failed to produce the strongest impression upon those whom she addressed." The explanation is superfluous; by failing to trust the effectiveness of the scene he has just created, Scott cancels much of its power.

Less striking but more natural is Dandie Dinmont, who was admired by more discriminating readers. To the *Edinburgh Review*, Dinmont was "the best rustic portrait that has ever yet been exhibited . . . the most honourable to rustics . . . the truest to nature, the most complete in all its lineaments." [2] Certainly Dinmont is the most complex character of the novel (but far from complex by later standards). His forthright energy in action and speech immediately win sympathy, and new aspects of his character are revealed as the novel progresses. An example is the contempt for hypocrisy he displays at the funeral of the elderly Miss Bertram (from whom he has hopes of a small legacy). As the ostentatiously grieving relatives dispute about who should carry the coffin, Dinmont loudly interrupts: "I think ye might hae at least gi'en me a leg o' her to carry . . . God! an it hadna been for the rigs o' land, I would hae gotten her a' to carry mysell, for as mony gentles as are here." It is difficult for the modern reader to realize the novelty of Dinmont; never in English fiction had such a character been presented so sympathetically, or at such length.

There is no need to consider the remaining characters closely. Dominie Sampson, the bore, is a bore indeed with his incredible absent-mindedness and his endlessly repeated "Pro-di-gious" (Scott's bores, pedants, and fools, who have a strong resemblance to one another, are usually constructed in a thoroughly mechanical fashion around some single "humour" or turn of speech). The heroines are—heroines; nothing more can be said, or needs to be. The primary hero, Brown-Bertram, arouses some interest as the plebeian Vanbeest Brown, who resents the "aristocratic oppression" of Colonel Mannering; but interest in Brown-Bertram diminishes when the novel reveals his identity as the missing Bertram heir. This sentence sums up his role: "Bertram, resolving to be passive in the hands of a person who had just rendered him such a distinguished piece of service, got into the chaise as directed." Scott makes a few efforts to enliven him, but without success. "By the knocking Nicholas! he'll plague, you, now he's come over the herring-pond. When he was so high, he had the spirit of thunder and lightning," Hatteraick tells Glossin (the principal villain, who has usurped the Bertram estate); but never is Brown-Bertram given any speech or action which would incline one to believe that description. It is simply his existence, rather than any act of his, that plagues Glossin.

The secondary hero, Hazlewood, is even dimmer. As for Hatteraick, the quotation above is a fair sample of his idiom. Glossin is simply a bully; a cad, (the triteness of the description matches the triteness of the characterization); and, according to convention, a coward. Scott does make an attempt at depth of characterization by presenting Glossin's "mental phantasmagoria" as he recalls his crimes, but the nightmare described is too prosaic and coherent to be convincing. The elder Bertram is credible as a self-important fool, but Scott destroys the characterization for the sake of a melodramatic scene when Bertram (who, to increase the pathos, has been made a helpless paralytic) exclaims during the sale of the family estate, at sight of Glossin: "Out of my sight, ye viper!—ye frozen viper, that I warmed till ye stung me!"

Guy Mannering, then, appears to be a "fluid pudding," in Henry James's phrase. It is a heap of adventures, melodrama, sometimes original and sometimes hackneyed characters, heavy English and lively Scots dialogue, plus much miscellaneous lore about the Scottish countryside. Its comparative failure enables us to see more clearly how much *Waverley* owed to its subject, the conflict of Jacobite and Hanoverian (but with implications so much wider), which gave it weight and unity.

But *Guy Mannering* may have, as a recent critic has suggested, its own interest as a kind of ideological novel, fantastic as this term may appear when applied to a novel by Scott. The ideology involved is that of property, honor, status, and gentlemanliness—topics inextricably connected with each other. It is primarily status, not power or wealth (though wealth is indispensable), that the hero of this, and of every Scott novel, eventually receives. As Lucy Bertram and her restored brother look toward the "seat of their ancestors," Lucy remarks: "God knows, my dear brother, I do not covert in your behalf the extensive power which the owners of these ruins are said to have possessed so long, and sometimes to have used so ill. But, oh, that I might see you in possession of such relics of their fortune as should give you an honorable independence." The hero is successively deprived of his true name and then even of his false one ("Vanbeest Brown"), of his military rank, of his money—in short, of all identity. Until his true birth is revealed, there is simply no place for him in the essentially static and highly structured society of the novel.

Welsh hardly exaggerates when he remarks that "most of the characters in *Guy Mannering* are set up by their author as checks and definitions of rank." Thus, "Sir Robert Hazlewood is a born gentleman, but fails the test of true modesty and minimal good sense." Lucy Bertram, on the other hand, triumphantly passes the test by her accomplishments, her modesty, and her patient enduring of misfortune. As for the hero, he is of course a gentleman by definition and is, for example, instantly recognized as such by Dandie Dinmont. But the perfect gentleman of the novel, in appearance, manners, and feelings, is Colonel Mannering. He is of "handsome, tall, thin figure," with "cast of features grave and interesting, and his air somewhat military. Every point of his appearance and address bespoke the gentleman." The ideal profession for a gentleman is military service; it is significant that Brown-Bertram, although ignorant of his birth, instinctively abandons commerce and possible wealth when the opportunity of a military career is offered.

Like Dinmont, the lower-class characters of the novel (even Meg, the gypsy), dearly love a lord; and, for them, the fall of the Bertram family and the sale of Ellangowan is a catastrophe even though it in no way affects them directly. The social hierarchy, for them, is the source of order and stability; and the fate of the great families provides a vicarious romance. The whole countryside seems to have an intense interest in the restoration of the heir of Ellangowan (Brown-Bertram) to his rightful estate.

As might be expected, the attitude of the two villains, Hatteraick and Glossin, contrasts sharply with this devotion to the principle of social hierarchy. When dealing with a person of higher status, Hatteraick is sullen, insolent, or offensively familiar. Clearly he either does not know his place in the scale, or he resents it and refuses to accept it. Glossin, on the other hand, accepts the hierarchy, but wishes to rise above his proper level. But his manner constantly betrays the false gentleman; he lacks completely the gentleman's sense of honor and his politeness toward those weaker than himself. Glossin alternately blusters and cringes. Faced with a true gentleman, such as Colonel Mannering, he abjectly retreats, even though in a physical contest he might very well win, being younger and stronger. Moreover, his society refuses to accept his pretensions. In the world of the novel, not all of Glossin's ill-gotten wealth can buy the status he craves or gain him acceptance as one of the gentlemen of his district. One says "In the world of the novel" because it seems probable that in the England of Scott's day the Glossins often reached their goal. Certainly *Guy Mannering* foreshadows the preoccupation of so much Victorian fiction with the question of who is and who is not a gentleman or a lady, and with what criteria (besides wealth) gentlemanliness may be determined. One does not have to credit Scott with a deliberate intention of exploring the ideology of status—which would appear highly improbable—to agree that the novel is almost a "treatise on real and pretended gentlemen." [3]

II The Antiquary

After a short period of uncertainty, *The Antiquary* (1816) equaled the success of its two predecessors; and no wonder, for it is very much the mixture as before, even to the point of repeating the missing-heir motif. The original Advertisement claims that "The present work completes a series of fictitious narratives intended to illustrate the manners of Scotland at three different periods," and the claim contains obvious truth. *Waverley* presented the Scotland of 1745, *Guy Mannering* that of about 1780; the period of *The Antiquary* is 1793 or 1794. Considering Scott's methods of work, however, and his aversion to planning, the implication that he had deliberately composed a kind of historical triptych seems unlikely. The background of the French Revolution and of the war between England and France provides occasional matter for conversation, but it does not seriously affect the action.

Before Lovel is revealed to be Geraldin Neville, son of the Earl of Glenallan, Scott provides an abundance of adventure: Lovel fights a duel with the Antiquary's fiery young nephew, Hector; treasure hunts by night in a ruined abbey are undertaken by the swindling Dousterswivel and his dupe, Sir Arthur Wardour; Sir Arthur and his daughter Isabella narrowly escape being drowned when they are trapped between the rising tide and a high cliff; a ghost appears to Lovel when he sleeps in the Antiquary's supposedly haunted room (Scott characteristically allows either a natural or a supernatural explanation of Lovel's vision). On the whole, Scott's complaint that *The Antiquary* "wants the romance of *Waverley* and the adventure of *Guy Mannering*" [4] because "the period did not admit of so much romantic situation" [5] seems unjustified.

The variety of character is even greater than the variety of incident. Jonathan Oldbuck, the antiquary, is the most effective of the upper-class characters. Although he has the pedantry of Baron Bradwardine, he is in no sense an imitation of the earlier character. He lacks the dignity and touch of heroism of Bradwardine, and has an individual strain of sardonic humor. Probably too much space is given to his antiquarian discourses, but Scott seldom knew when he had done enough. The hero and heroine are, if possible, less individualized than before. Indeed, the reader never even learns the first name of the hero! Lovel is introduced on the opening page as "a young man of genteel appearance," and the phrase sums him up quite adequately. The heroine, usually referred to as Miss Wardour (though she does have a first name), is as ladylike as Lovel is genteel and possesses a "tall and elegant figure." One knows, and needs to know, nothing more about her. The hero, who disappears for two hundred pages, returns at the conclusion to be united to the heroine and his newly discovered father; but his absence is hardly noticed.

The English dialogue is as stilted as ever (except in some of Oldbuck's speeches), and the narrative and descriptive prose are as heavy and long-winded. "Here, then," Scott writes when Lovel, Miss Wardour, and her father are trapped by the rising tide, "They were to await the slow though sure progress of the raging element, something in the situation of the martyrs of the early church, who, exposed by heathen tyrants to be slain by wild beasts, were compelled for a time to witness the impatience and rage by which the animals were agitated, while awaiting the signal for undoing their grates, and letting them lose upon the victims." The simile, inappropriate and obtrusive, destroys whatever tension has been created. Sometimes the diction is incorrect, as when Scott precedes an analysis of the antiquary's state of mind with, "Were I compelled to decompose [sic] the motives of my worthy friend."

Again the Scots dialogue of the lower-class characters might be the work of a different novelist. How they talk! Wit, vivid imagery, pathos, poetry, can all be found. "He's but a brunt crust," remarks a woman of Sir Arthur Wardour, who is rumored to be bankrupt. An innkeeper remarks, in all seriousness, of a "ganging plea" concerning the boundary of his backyard, which he had inherited from his father and grandfather: "Oh, it's a beautiful thing to see how lang and how carefully justice is considered in this country!" Edie Ochiltree, the wandering beggar, provides a kind of apology for his life: "And then what wad a' the country about do for want o' auld Edie Ochiltree, that brings news and country cracks frae farm-steading to anither, and gingerbread to the lasses, and helps the lads to mend their fiddles, and the gude-wives to clout their pans . . . and has skill o' cow-ills and horse-ills, and kens mair auld sangs and tales than a' the barony besides, and gars ilka body laugh wherever he comes?" Or there is the answer of old Mucklebackit, the fisherman, after the death of his son, as he explains to Oldbuck why he must repair his boat: "And what would you have me to do, unless I wanted to see four children starve, because one is drowned? It's weel wi' you gentles, that can sit in the house wi' handkerchers at your een, when ye lose a friend; but the like o' us maun to our work again, if our hearts were beating as hard as my hammer."

There are some brief but concrete and finely imagined scenes of village life; for example, the wake for Steenie Mucklebackit or the neighborhood gossips examining the mail at the post office and blackening the characters of its recipients. Scott himself was aware of where his greatest strength as a novelist lay; in the Advertisement he remarks that in both *Guy Mannering* and in *The Antiquary* he has sought his "principal personages" among the lower class, which is "the last to feel the influence of that general polish which assimilates to each other the manners of different nations. Among the same class I have placed some of the scenes, in which I have endeavoured to illustrate the operation of the higher and more violent passions; both because the lower orders are less restrained by the habit of suppressing their feelings, and because I agree with my friend Wordsworth, that they seldom fail to express them in the strongest and most powerful language." Unfortunately, these characters are not really, except for Edie Ochiltree, the principal personages; and, excepting Ochiltree and

also the melodramatic Elspeth Mucklebackit, they are at best peripheral to the main action of the novel; they often are entirely
irrelevant.

The only twentieth-century critic who has given serious attention to *The Antiquary* is E. M. Forster in *Aspects of the Novel*.
His general critique of Scott will be considered later, but his devastating summary of the plot (or "story," as Forster prefers to call
it) of *The Antiquary* cannot be ignored here. Unfortunately this
amusing précis is too long to quote, but Forster's point is that
there is no causal sequence, such as forms a true plot, to be discovered among the story's happenings, that the only principle of
construction is to introduce new characters and new episodes
which keep the reader's curiosity alive. Irrelevancies, loose ends,
and false scents are numerous; but Scott can count on the reader's
absent-mindedness to overlook or forget them. Forster comments
on the description of the storm which endangers the hero and
heroine: "The rocks are of cardboard . . . the tempest is turned
on with one hand while Scott scribbles away about Early Christians with the other; there is no sincerity, no sense of danger in the
whole affair; it is all passionless, perfunctory; yet we do just want
to know what happens next." And this desire to know keeps the
reader turning the pages until the story is concluded by the "idi-
otic finale" of marriage and by a final page or two in which the
reader's moral sense is satisfied with the customary "distribution
of prizes, pensions, husbands, wives, babies, millions, appended
paragraphs, and cheerful remarks." [6]

One might argue that Forster's method of summary could be
used to prove any novel ridiculous, but it can hardly be denied
that he is justified in asserting that the principal interest of the
story depends on the author's "primitive power of keeping the
reader in suspense and playing on his curiosity." And the questions constantly raised in the novel are of the kind which, once
answered, completely cease to interest the intelligent reader. Such
a reader will not be much concerned a second time with the problem of how the treasure came to be hidden in the ruined abbey
or with the mystery of Lovel's identity.

But Forster is mistaken when he says that *all* the novel has to
offer is the satisfaction of a rather crude curiosity. It also has, in
Lockhart's words, "a kind of simple unsought charm" which de-

rives entirely from "the humbler and softer scenes, the transcript of actual Scottish life." [7] This charm resides principally in the vernacular speech of the lower-class characters, and it provides an attraction as powerful as the suspense created by the story. One wishes that this living part of the work could be cut away from the dead weight of the hero and heroine and everything that concerns them; but, even in so loosely structured a novel as *The Antiquary,* such a separation is impossible.

CHAPTER 6

Old Mortality

IN December, 1816—six months after the publication of *The Antiquary*—*Tales of My Landlord, First Series* (including *Old Mortality* and *The Black Dwarf*) appeared. Scott's original intention had been to write four short novels, each filling a volume and each set in a different district of Scotland; but, as Lockhart remarks, "his imagination once kindled upon any theme, he could not but pour himself out freely—so that notion was soon abandoned." [1] *Old Mortality* was stretched, therefore, to the customary three-volume length.

Its predecessor, *The Antiquary*, had come closest to the contemporary scene; *Old Mortality* represented Scott's deepest plunge into the past up to that time; its action covers the period 1679–89. When Scott began *Waverley* he had been dealing with events "sixty years since." This difference between *Waverley* and *Old Mortality* is significant: in the former novel he had drawn heavily, both for episodes and for his general sense of the period, on the stories he had heard from elderly survivors; but no such sources existed for *Old Mortality*. The author was compelled to rely entirely on the knowledge which he had gained from historical studies, from the seventeenth-century pamphlets which he had edited, and from traditions reported to him by others. To base a novel on such material is difficult, and represents a common cause of failure in historical fiction. Often the novel is too barely furnished to provide the detailed realism necessary for the illusion of fiction, or at the opposite extreme it may be packed with undigested facts apparently transferred directly from the author's note cards. In *Old Mortality*, on the whole, Scott avoids both extremes; the world he creates is solid and convincing, yet there is seldom any pedantic display of information for its own sake. Scott was confident, writes Lockhart, "that the industry with which he had

pored over a library of forgotten tracts would enable him to iden-
tify himself with the time in which they had birth, as completely
as if he had listened with his own ears to the dismal sermons of
Peden, ridden with Claverhouse and Dalzell in the rout of Bothwell, and been an advocate at the bar of the Privy Council," [2] and
his confidence was justified.

I   A Divided Country

Although the subject of *Old Mortality*—the rebellion of the
Covenanters which was defeated at Bothwell Bridge in 1679—
was suggested by chance to Scott, it seems an inevitable choice. It
offered the opportunity for that dramatic contrast of strikingly
different cultures in which Scott delighted. Here, however, the
contrast was not between Lowlanders and Highlanders, but between Cavaliers and Covenanters, opposed elements of the same
society. "There are noble subjects for narrative during that period," Scott commented, "full of the strongest light and shadow,
all human passions stirr'd up and stimulated by the most powerful
motives and the contending parties as distinctly contrasted in
manners and in modes of thinking as in political principles." [3]

The opening chapter, although marred somewhat by the rather
tiresome and inappropriate facetiousness of the fictitious Jedediah
Cleishbotham (the landlord of *Tales of My Landlord*), estab-
lishes the somber tone of the novel and indicates the balance
which the narrator hopes to achieve in writing of long-dead con-
troversies: "If recollection of former injuries, extra-loyalty, and
contempt and hatred of their adversaries, produced rigour and
tyranny in the one party, it will hardly be denied, on the other
hand, that, if the zeal for God's house did not eat up the conven-
ticlers, it devoured at least . . . no small portion of their loyalty,
sober sense, and good breeding." The figure of Old Mortality, a
real historical personage who in a peaceful age devoted his life to
preserving the memory of the "killing times" by cleansing the epi-
taphs of the Presbyterian martyrs, suggests that the purpose of the
author himself was to revive the memory of the past more effectively than Old Mortality ever could. The sources from which the
narrator claims to have gathered his information—traditions reported by small farmers, pedlars, country weavers, tailors—indicate the popular nature of the Presbyterian cause.

The following two chapters, devoted to the *wappenschaw* or gathering of militia with the accompanying sports and military exercises, provide a detailed account of obsolete Scottish customs; and, more importantly, they give the reader the sense of a bitterly divided country in which every event gains a political significance. The *wappenschaw* is intended partly as a display of the armed force of the "aristocratical" party supporting the king and episcopalianism and partly as a deliberate outrage of the puritanical scruples of the Covenanters. Further, it is an attempt by the government "to revive those feudal institutions which united the vassal to the liege lord, and both to the crown." The attempt was unsuccessful, as Scott points out, for the ironic consequence is that "the youth of both sexes, to whom the pipe and tabor in England, or the bagpipe in Scotland, would have been in themselves an irresistible temptation, were enabled to set them at defiance, from the proud consciousness that they were, at the same time, resisting an act of council," while "The rigour of the strict Calvinists increased, in proportion to the wishes of the government that it should be relaxed."

Arising from the effort of Charles II to establish his authority over the Scottish church by instituting an Episcopalian form of church government (with bishops appointed by the Crown) and also from the brutal persecution of those who attended services conducted by their own, unauthorized ministers, the dispute had broadened to become a class struggle. The aristocracy of Scotland was arrayed on one side and on the other, the great majority of the peasantry, as well as the small middle class and some of the minor landlords. The conflict was also national, for it was against a foreign (English) church organization. Between the two sides lay an uneasy body of moderates who deplored the cruelty and fanaticism of both extremes, or who simply hoped to remain neutral and avoid trouble. The aristocratic party possessed a monopoly of organized military force; but its complete lack of support among the people and its essential hollowness are comically revealed by Lady Bellenden's raggle-taggle troop of militiamen consisting of "the fowler and falconer, the footman, and the ploughman at the home farm, with an old drunken cavaliering butler," an ancient steward, and Guse Gibbie, the village half-wit.

In such a society—divided on lines of class, religion, and political opinion—the position of the moderate is difficult. The long speech of advice by Niel Blane, the innkeeper, to his daughter, dramatizes both the condition of the country and the problems of the non-political man who wishes to do business with Whig and Tory. Blane's moderation is based on common sense and good-humored selfishness, but that of Henry Morton, the hero of the novel, derives from reason and principle—and his position is accordingly more uncomfortable. Both parties watch Morton carefully and hope for his support, but he is too much aware of the faults of each. "Can I be a man, and a Scotchman, and look with indifference on that persecution which has made wise men mad?" Morton asks. Then he checks himself with another question: "Who shall warrant me that these people, rendered wild by persecution, would not, in the hour of victory, be as cruel and as intolerant as those by whom they are now hunted down?" Morton concludes by rejecting both sides: "I am weary of seeing nothing but violence and fury around me—now assuming the mask of lawful authority, now taking that of religious zeal."

Sick of his frustration and inaction, of his dependence on his miserly uncle, of his apparently hopeless love for Edith Bellenden, Morton resolves to win his way as a soldier of fortune on the Continent: "My father's sword is mine, and Europe lies open before me." But, like most Scott heroes, he is eloquent in making resolutions and slow in carrying them out; he is easily discouraged from executing his plan.

Meanwhile, Morton has already become unwittingly involved on the side of the Covenanters by giving aid to Balfour of Burley, whom he knows as his father's old comrade, but who is also the fleeing assassin of Archbishop Sharp, head of the Scottish Church. Burley, a militant fanatic, is a far more compelling figure than the moderate and rational hero; and in their debate Morton certainly gets the worst of it. For Burley, the faithful are required not to submit passively to martyrdom but to draw the sword and "smite the ungodly." Morton's abstract language is appropriate to the moral commonplaces he utters: "I own I should doubt the origin of any inspiration which seemed to dictate a line of conduct contrary to those feelings of natural humanity, which Heaven has assigned to us as the general law of our conduct." Burley also speaks standard English, but his diction, abounding in active verbs, is vigorous and concrete: "I say unto you, that all communication with the enemies of the Church is the accursed thing which God hateth! Touch not—taste not—handle not!"

A different aspect of the Presbyterian spirit is represented by old Mause, the mother of Morton's servant, Cuddie. With her defiance of Lady Margaret Bellenden, at the cost of being turned out of her farm, she displays a comic heroism, and her scriptural language neatly parodies that of Burley. Her enthusiasm (in the eighteenth-century sense) is brought out sharply by the contrast with Cuddie's practical shrewdness and by her conflicting desires for the spiritual and physical welfare of Cuddie. His spiritual welfare would, of course, be best served if he publicly "testified" and became a martyr.

The arrival of the king's dragoons at the house of old Milnwood, Morton's uncle, provides Scott with the opportunity for one of the longest, most fully developed scenes in the novel. The scene is set with a detailed description of Milnwood's dinner, at which all the household take part, for "The Laird of Milnwood kept up all old fashions which were connected with economy." The details of the coarse food and thin beer reveal both the "manners" of the time and the extreme avarice of Milnwood. The dinner is dramatically interrupted by a pounding at the gate and by the noisy entry of the dragoons, with the clatter of their iron boots on the stone floor and the clash of their huge swords. Scott quickly summarizes the attitude of each character: old Milnwood's fear of extortion; Morton's apprehension because he has aided a rebel; Mause Headrigg's quandary "between fear for her son's life and an overstrained and enthusiastic zeal, which reproached her for consenting even tacitly to belie her religious sentiments"; and Cuddie's quick use of the confusion to give himself an extra helping of soup.

The prevailing tone at first is of rough good humor, as the soldiers compel the reluctant Milnwood to supply them with claret and brandy and to propose toasts to the king as a test of loyalty. The good humor changes instantly to brutal ferocity when Morton questions the authority of Sergeant Bothwell to examine him and when Bothwell replies fiercely: "You ask me for the right to examine you, sir . . . my cockade and my broad-sword are my commission." Morton's scrupulous honesty in admitting his association with Burley incriminates him; but he abruptly refuses to answer further questions. The climax of the scene appears to have arrived when Bothwell threatens torture, and then the tension seems to relax as Milnwood offers the troopers a bribe, which Bothwell accepts. But Scott has not finished yet; we had forgotten old Mause, but as the sergeant begins to administer an oath of loyalty to the household, she can no longer be restrained and breaks out in a furious denunciation of the soldiers: "Malignant adherents ye are to the prelates, foul props to a feeble and filthy cause, bloody beasts of prey, and burdens to the earth." Morton is led away by Bothwell's men, who cannot overlook Mause's outburst; and the scene ends with the expulsion of the Headriggs from the estate of Milnwood and with the housekeeper's angry judgment of Mause: "Ill-fard, crazy, crack-brained gowk that she is! to set up to be sae muckle better than ither folk, the auld besom.'

The scene itself is admirably managed; it is an ensemble in which Bothwell, Milnwood, Morton, the Headriggs, and the housekeeper all are given opportunity to act and speak fully and characteristically. Each, too, has his own style: there is the shrill repetitiousness of Mause ("I wad persevere, natheless, in lifting my testimony against popery, prelacy, antinomianism, erastianism, lapsarianism, sublapsarianism, and the sins and snares of the times"); the almost poetic level of rhythm and emotional intensity which the old miser Milnwood reaches in his agony at risking both his nephew and his money, "O, the lands of Milnwood!—the bonny lands of Milnwood, that have been in the name of Morton twa hundred years! they are barking and fleeing, outfield and infield, haugh and holme!"; the insolent familiarity of Bothwell; and the standard English, as correct as his sentiments, of the hero. The prevailingly comic tone assures the reader that nothing tragic will occur—old Mause will not be taken out and shot; the hero will not really be tortured—but the comedy is of that nervous kind which rests on apprehension. The mood, however, is carefully varied; tension is high at the entrance of the soldiers, gradually relaxes as they drink Milnwood's liquor, heightens as Morton questions their authority and refuses to reveal the whereabouts of Burley, eases once more as Milnwood offers his bribe, then suddenly rises again as Mause interrupts with her general denunciation. The reader has waited uneasily for Mause to speak up, hoping that she will remain quiet but not really expecting it. Her carefully delayed outburst dramatically reverses mood and action, and leads to Morton's arrest.

Morton is carried before Claverhouse, the royal commander, at Lady Margaret Bellenden's castle of Tillietudlem (the heavy comedy, indicated even by the name "Tillietudlem," of Lady Margaret and her exaggerated loyalty form the weakest element of the novel). An interview, intended to be passionate, occurs between Morton and Edith Bellenden, who is even more absurd than a Scott heroine generally is in her scruples about visiting Morton in his imprisonment: "I have taken a strange step, Mr. Morton—a step that perhaps may expose me to censure in your eyes—But I have long permitted you to use the language of friendship—perhaps I might say more—too long to leave you when the world seems to have left you." But the love affair and Morton's rivalry with Lord Evandale, a royalist, are of no serious interest. No relationships described in such language as the following could be of interest: "Edith was touched by the hopeless and reverential passion of the gallant youth who now took leave of her to rush into dangers of no ordinary description" (referring to Evandale, who is marching off to fight the Covenanters). The abstractness of the language—"hopeless and reverential passion"—the triteness of "gallant youth" and the flat anticlimax of "dangers of no ordinary description" nullify the intended effect.

Brought before Claverhouse, Morton refuses to defend himself; and Scott apparently had forgotten that Morton earlier had relied on Claverhouse's soldierly nature to listen with favor to a "blunt, unvarnished defence." Morton denies the authority of Claverhouse to examine him, and is condemned to instant execution, but is saved by the intercession of Evandale. Scott tries to impress the reader through Claverhouse's fears with Morton's potential danger to the state: "His father was positively the most dangerous man in all Scotland, cool, resolute, soldierly, and inflexible in his cursed principles. His son seems his very model; you cannot conceive the mischief he may do." Indeed, one cannot; the reader has seen too much of Morton to believe him the most dangerous man in Scotland, no matter how many adjectives Claverhouse applies.

Carried off once more by the troopers, Morton meets Cuddie

Headrigg, old Mause's son, who has been arrested for hearing a field-preacher. Scott attempts a double plot, with Cuddie's love for Jenny Dennison, Edith Bellenden's maid, and his rivalry with the trooper Tam Halliday providing a comic parallel with the relationships of Morton, Edith, and Evandale. Unfortunately, the contrast merely makes the hero and heroine more lifeless. As prisoner, Morton witnesses the Battle of Loudon-hill in which Burley and the Whigs defeat the overconfident dragoons. The battle scene itself, with its realism, detail, and absence of heroics, is the best thing of its kind in Scott or in English fiction to that time.

Morton is freed by the victorious rebels. Outraged by the injustices committed on himself and others and having no alternative, he finally chooses a side and joins the Covenanters. He does not prove, however, the fiery inciter and leader of rebellion that Claverhouse's words might have led the reader to expect. His first action is to rescue Evandale from a general massacre of prisoners, and his principal effort at the ensuing siege of Tillietudlem is to prevent the rebels from injuring any of the Bellendens. Characteristically, his doubts begin as soon as he has committed himself; he finds himself "better satisfied with the general justice of the cause he had espoused, than either with the measures or the motives of many of those who were embarked in it" (a comment that probably could be made with equal justification about any revolution in history). The cause is too extreme and too democratic for a genteel Scott hero to feel comfortable among its supporters. But, if Morton's part is almost entirely negative, Scott makes good use of him as an observer. The novel discriminates precisely between the enthusiasm of Burley, tempered by his ambition and his recognition of the need for unity; the pure zeal of Macbriar, admirable yet frightening, untainted by practical or worldly considerations; and the bloodthirsty fanaticism of the half-insane Habbakuk Mucklewrath—"Who speaks of mercy to the bloody house of the malignants? I say take the infants and dash them against the stones; take the daughters and the mothers of the house and hurl them from the battlements of their trust, that the dogs may fatten on their blood." The councils of the Whigs show the factionalism typical of ideological revolutions, in which, as Scott observes, "it seemed likely that those of the most violent opinions were, as usual in such cases, to possess and exert the greater degree of energy." Morton, the moderate man who "would willingly terminate this war without any bloody victory," is ineffectual and out of place. In considering possible eventualities, defeat always occurs to him first. Occasionally Scott reminds the hero and the reader "that, engaged as he was in a perilous cause, it was absolutely necessary that he should conquer or die," but one is not convinced that Morton will do either; in the outcome he does not.

Morton, present at an unsuccessful attack on Tillietudlem, marches with the main body of the rebels to Glasgow but returns to Tillietudlem in time to save Evandale's life a second time and to secure the surrender of the castle and the safety of its inmates. He then carries out a useless peace mission to the Duke of Monmouth, commander of the royal forces. The rebel army, divided within itself, is routed at Bothwell Bridge. Morton, during his escape, falls in with a band of extreme fanatics, including Macbriar and Mucklewrath. Eager for a scapegoat, they conduct a drumhead trial and sentence Morton to death; his crimes are his efforts to aid personal friends among the royalists and to win honorable terms of peace from Monmouth. Morton is to die at midnight since the Covenanters will not shed his blood on the Sabbath; but, as Mucklewrath in his impatience is about to set the clock ahead, Claverhouse's troopers arrive on the gallop, kill or capture the Whigs, and rescue Morton. Because of his aristocratic birth, he is treated with respect by Claverhouse; but the captured Whigs are led out to instant execution.

Morton comes to recognize a parallel between Claverhouse and Burley because of the zeal and ruthlessness of each. And Claverhouse readily admits: "You are very right—we are both fanatics; but there is some distinction between the fanaticism of honour and that of dark and sullen superstition." The "fanaticism of honor" leads to an admirable disinterested courage, but also to the most callous indifference to the lives of others—at least to those of the lower classes. Acknowledging that both he and Burley shed blood "without mercy or remorse," Claverhouse justifies himself: "Surely . . . but of what kind?—There is a difference, I trust, between the blood of learned and reverend prelates and scholars, of gallant soldiers and noble gentlemen, and the red puddle that stagnates in the veins of psalm-singing mechanics, crack-brained demagogues, and sullen boors."

Morton's helplessness as a prisoner brings him a paradoxical relief: "His hours flowed on less anxiously than at any time since his having commenced actor in public life. He was now, with respect to his fortune, like a rider who has flung his reins on the horse's neck, and, while he abandoned himself to circumstances, was at least relieved from the task of attempting to direct them." But Scott fails to realize that essentially, but less obviously, this situation has been Morton's throughout the novel; indeed, it is the typical position of the Scott hero. Morton is brought before the Privy Council, but it has been arranged in advance by Claverhouse that he will get off with a sentence of exile. Scott takes advantage of Morton's presence to show Macbriar resisting questioning and torture. The scene is striking, but at some cost. As an early critic observed, "The contrast of Henry Morton, pardoned by the government and pursuing his fortune in Holland, with Macbriar tortured and put to death, with Burley, a wanderer in the desert hills . . . is almost fatal to the romantic interest of his character." [4] The outraged Morton is *about* to intervene but, as usual, is prevented.

A gap of ten years follows, for Morton cannot return until after the triumph of his principles in the "glorious Revolution" of 1688. (Meanwhile, rather absurdly, he has become a major-general!) There is a genuine melancholy in the final chapters as he finds all changed, his uncle dead, himself believed drowned, and Edith Bellenden about to marry Evandale. A confused huddle of events follows, as Morton encounters the now half-mad Burley; is discovered by Edith, who breaks her engagement to Evandale; and learns of a plot by Burley against Evandale's life, but characteristically arrives too late to help. Burley and the villainous Basil Olifant, who has dispossessed the Bellendens of their property, are killed, however. In a concluding chapter, under the person of Jedediah Cleishbotham, Scott briefly summarizes the future lives of his characters; and the tone and manner of the dialogue between Cleishbotham and Miss Buskbody, an inveterate novel reader, indicate his consciousness of the fatuousness of this conventional requirement.

II *Assessment*

Old Mortality is often considered, with much justification, the finest of Scott's historical novels. Scott himself remarked, shortly after publication, "I really prefer [it] to any fictitious narrative I have yet been able to produce." [5] One notices first, no doubt, the ease and certainty with which a vanished world is recreated—certainly, as Lockhart remarks, the portrayal represents a greater feat of imagination than Scott had ever displayed in his poetry. One notes too the completeness of this world; every level of Lowland society is included. As the Marxist critic Georg Lukacs observed, "Like every great popular writer, Scott aims at portraying the totality of national life in its complex interaction between 'above' and 'below'." [6] The comment is just in general, but it applies particularly to *Old Mortality*. The novel is historical in the most profound sense: its characters are actively engaged in the making of history and their actions and their fortunes, even the outcome of their love affairs, are determined by historical events—in this case, the course of the rebellion. As a contemporary reviewer noted, Scott uses historical events "rather to develop the characters" of a novel "than for any purpose of political information"; and he creates a sense of the past "less by his direct notices of the great transactions . . . than by his casual intimations of their effects on private persons." [7] Historical errors and anachronisms, such as letting Claverhouse use the word "sentimental" some seventy years before it had entered the language, may occur; but their effect is insignificant. Scott even feels free to falsify history when necessary; thus, the historical Burley was not drowned in a Scotch river in 1689 but died at sea some time earlier while returning to Scotland from exile. Such manipulation of history for artistic purposes seems entirely legitimate as long as the reader's knowledge of historical fact is not outraged and the dramatic illusion thus disturbed.

But Scott is not merely concerned with rendering the past; he wishes to interpret it and relate it to what had gone before and to what followed. In other words, he had a philosophy of history—although he would hardly have used such a pretentious term. Like most Englishmen of his time, Scott was a believer in progress, but, with some inconsistency, he apparently believed that social and political progress had reached its end in his own age and that any further change would necessarily be for the worse. No doubt such feelings are common in every generation, but Scott's fear of change was irrational and extreme. He seems to conceive of British history as a "middle course, asserting itself between extremes" —in this case, the extremes of "Malignant" and Cameronian, akin to the Cavaliers and Roundheads of the English civil wars. In *Old Mortality* each extreme is personified in an individual leader, a Burley or a Claverhouse, a figure slightly larger than life who concentrates within himself the characteristic qualities of his party. Claverhouse, at least, is made to recognize the parallel when he admits to Morton that he and Burley are both fanatics. It may be added that in spite of contemporary attacks on his presentation of the Covenanters, Scott holds the balance fairly, even though his esthetic preference is plainly and quite naturally for Claverhouse, the polished gentleman.

As his hero, Scott characteristically chooses a figure who "may, through character and fortune, enter into human contact with both sides" [8] and so must not be a strong partisan of either. So Morton is brought into contact with the aristocratic party by his rank and with the Covenanters by his Presbyterian background. Although Morton finally takes a side, he does so only when no alternative is left. He is the most moderate of revolutionists, and his relief is genuine when his uncongenial role is ended by defeat and capture. David Daiches has called Morton an "intelligent liberal in a world of extremists." [9] Revolted by the excesses of both parties, he, like many liberals, is perhaps especially sensitive to the faults of his own side.

But, while the novel is dominated by Burley and Claverhouse, the future belongs to the colorless Morton. Although the complete victory of one extreme at Bothwell Bridge leaves no place in Scotland for Morton, the reader is aware that his principles will be established by the revolution of 1688; from it will evolve a more modern civilization, one free of cruelty, superstition, and fanaticism. Morton and Cuddie Headrigg adapt themselves to the new order and eventually flourish; Burley and Claverhouse cannot and die (Claverhouse's death in his useless victory at Killiecrankie is imminent as the novel concludes).

Despite the Toryism that displays itself in Scott's dislike of change in his own time and in his sympathy with Jacobitism and similar lost causes, Scott's view of British history—and particularly of the history of the seventeenth century—is the Whig one, which established itself as the standard interpretation during the nineteenth century. In its fundamentals, his outlook is not very different from that of Macaulay's *History of England*, although Scott's tolerance and wider range of sympathy perhaps enable the novelist to recreate the past more fairly and even more accurately than the historian could do.

Unfortunately, the character of Morton is not substantial enough to bear the significance that the structure and theme of the novel place on it. Like most of Scott's heroes, Morton has no real inner life, and Scott is quite unable to convince us of the changes supposed to be taking place within him. Morton is frequently *about* to act—he almost goes to Europe to become a soldier of fortune, he almost fights Bothwell in the tavern, he almost tries to stop the torture of Macbriar—but he seldom does. Scott uses a revealing simile to describe Morton's condition as he is first brought before Claverhouse for examination: "Desperate himself, he determined to support the rights of his country, insulted in his person. His character was for the moment as effectually changed as the appearance of a villa, which, from being the abode of domestic quiet and happiness, is, by the sudden intrusion of an armed force, converted into a formidable post of defence." But the change is only for the moment and, apparently, only in appearance. The suburban villa, with its connotations of domesticity, comfort, and bourgeois prosperity, provides a more apt comparison for Morton than Scott perhaps realized.

A second weakness is that Morton's whole character is an anachronism that disturbs the knowledgeable reader's sense of history far more seriously than Claverhouse's use of "sentimental." Morton simply does not belong in the same world as Burley and Macbriar, or as Claverhouse and Bothwell. Morton's rational Christianity; his lack of concern with matters of church government, order of service, or even doctrine; and his devotion to law, order, and a strictly limited freedom make him an eighteenth-century figure who is misplaced in the seventeenth. He belongs rightly in the Scotland of David Hume and Adam Smith; no wonder he is uncomfortable in that of Claverhouse and Burley. This weakness Scott himself may not have realized, for his understanding of the period was, after all, limited. Scott could present the Cameronians strikingly and in detail; but he could not fully understand them because the issues for which they fought were, for him, trivial or ridiculous. This deficiency is serious, for part of his business as novelist is to make his readers understand why these questions were literally matters of life and death for those involved. This lack of understanding is shown by a later comment: "They [Covenanters and Malignants] were both a set of cruel and bloody bigots, and had, notwithstanding, those virtues with which bigotry is sometimes allied. Their characters were of a kind much more picturesque than beautiful . . . so far as they can be distinguished from each other, one is tempted to hate most the party which chances to be uppermost for the time." [10] Indeed, they are picturesque as *Old Mortality* presents them; but that picturesqueness is gained at the heavy cost of a certain superficiality in both characterization and historical insight.

CHAPTER 7

Three Other Novels

I Rob Roy

*R*OB ROY, published in January, 1818, enjoyed an even greater immediate success than its predecessors: it sold ten thousand copies within two weeks. For many good judges, writes Buchan, "it has been the favorite among the novels." [1] Consequently, although it shows no development in technique and introduces no novelties of theme or characterization, it cannot be passed over entirely.

The action of the novel occurs in 1715 and is concerned closely with the unsuccessful Jacobite rising of that year. Frank Osbaldistone, the hero, resembles Waverley; he has a taste for romance and dabbles in poetry. His refusal to enter his father's business precipitates the action. His father, devoted to business (more accurately to speculation) and having a supreme contempt for poetry, packs him off to the family seat at Osbaldistone Hall in the north of England; intending to replace him in the firm with his cousin Rashleigh. With Sir Hildebrand Osbaldistone and his loutish sons—all of whom live for drink, Jacobitism, and field sports—Frank exists in a boredom somewhat relieved by the company of the villainous but intellectual Rashleigh and of the beautiful, mysterious, unconventional Diana Vernon. Rashleigh eventually goes to London, is left in full charge of the business while the elder Osbaldistone travels to Holland, and absconds with the firm's assets (the nature of these is never very clearly specified). To regain the assets and to save the house of Osbaldistone and Tresham from ruin, Frank follows Rashleigh to Glasgow and fights a duel with him that is interrupted just before a fatal result. With Bailie Nicol Jarvie, a business associate of his father, Frank journeys to the Highlands in search of the missing papers. There he is impressed with the scenery (described at considerable length), watches the defeat of some royal troops by the clan of the famous outlaw Rob Roy Macgregor, is captured and released, witnesses the escape of Rob Roy from his captors, and encounters Diana Vernon in the company of an unknown gentleman whom Frank assumes to be her husband or lover (actually her father). Because of the influence of Rob Roy, who has taken a liking for him, and of Diana, the papers are eventually returned to Frank and the Osbaldistone business is saved. Resolving to enter the business after all, Frank returns to England just as the Jacobite rising breaks out. Sir Hildebrand and five of his sons join the rising and die; Rashleigh, who has turned informer, is killed by Rob Roy. Frank inherits Osbaldistone Hall and marries Diana Vernon.

Even a brief analysis indicates that *Rob Roy* has been overpraised. The opening sections, like those of *Waverley*, have been generally considered as inferior. As Buchan comments, "The tale only finds its true key when Frank, with Andrew Fairservice as his Sancho Panza, rides off in the darkness for the north. Thereafter we are in the grip of epic narrative." [2] But over two hundred pages pass before "the tale finds its true key"! This opening half is extremely thin, probably because Scott did not know and could not or did not imagine the characters and the scene he describes. Sir Hildebrand is a rather incongruous combination of Squire Western and Sir Roger de Coverley, and the five cousins are hardly characterized at all. Life at Osbaldistone Hall simply is not realized in the novel: it is never there for the reader to *see;* it is only briefly and vaguely described.

The plot, loose and episodic, contains a damaging flaw. In order to get the hero into the Highlands, Scott arranges for Rashleigh to steal the Osbaldistone assets. An unconvincing attempt is made, therefore, to connect this act with Rashleigh's role as a Jacobite agent—by ruining the Osbaldistone firm he will prevent it from paying debts to various Highland chiefs, thus increasing economic distress and making the Highlands more receptive to rebellion. But much worse is the senior Osbaldistone's action in leaving Rashleigh in full charge of affairs for a period of weeks. Osbaldistone has been presented as a hard, shrewd businessman who has a keen insight into character and who is always watchful of his own interests, but Rashleigh would arouse suspicion at first sight in any reasonable person. Frank had written earlier: "Although I did feel a certain qualm of conscience at having been the means of introducing Rashleigh . . . into my father's business—perhaps his confidence—I subdued it by the reflection that my father was complete master of his own affairs—a man not to be imposed upon, or influenced by anyone." Frank expresses precisely the impression that the reader has formed. Consequently, the event is simply incredible; Scott makes his characters behave, for the sake of his plot, in a way absolutely contradictory to their nature. And what Coleridge called "the daydream of negative faith," the necessary illusion of fiction, receives a shock from which it is not likely to recover. Nowhere could one find a better illustration of Coleridge's remark that "Scott's great defect" is that "nothing is evolved out of the character or passions of the agent; but all is accident *ab extra.*" [3]

The hero of *Rob Roy* is simply a genteel young man with literary inclinations (but this aspect of his characterization is soon neglected), and he is in no way distinguishable from most other Scott heroes. The heroine, however, at first appears to differ strikingly from her counterparts in the other novels. She is described as forthright, unconventional, passionate, and witty; and generations of male readers have appropriately fallen in love with her. "Whatever she says or does, we are her devout henchmen, believing fiercely in her beauty, her goodness and her brains." [4] Such readers, however, have perhaps mistaken intention for accomplishment. Diana's speech gives her away, and often completely belies the intended effect: "No, no Rashleigh, dismiss from your company the false archimage Dissimulation, and it will better ensure your free access to our classical consultations." Leslie Fiedler's damaging comment seems justified: she is not really the incarnation of romance that she seems, but "only the Good-Bad girl, that stock character of popular fiction. . . . Did she not persuade Frank from the pursuit of poetry, sending him back to protect his father's interests?" [5] The villainous Rashleigh, who has acted as Diana's tutor, instructed her in philosophy, mathematics, and astronomy (needless to say, her conversation gives no evidence of such knowledge); and he later attempted to seduce her. The hero's comment is worth quoting: her "profound studies" seemed "more fitted for a churchman than for a beautiful female"; and Rashleigh's purpose in engaging her in such abstruse topics must have been "to break down and confound in her mind the difference and distinction between the sexes, and to habituate her to trains of subtle reasoning, by which he might at his own time invest that which is wrong with the colour of that which is right." It may be reasonably assumed that this exquisitely complacent sense of male superiority and the absurdly conventional view of woman's proper education belong to Scott himself, as well as to his hero. It would be difficult to find a passage which reveals more clearly Scott's intellectual limitations and the conventionality of his thought.

What serious significance the novel possesses is contained in the Highland-Lowland contrast. Here, as in *Waverley*, the Highlands are Catholic, Jacobite, violent, and lawless; the Lowlands, Protestant, Whiggish, legalistic, and commercial. This contrast is also one of past and future. Scott's clear comprehension of the actual historical situation is revealed without moralizing, or romanticizing, in Bailie Nichol Jarvie's long account of the Highlands to Frank that is based entirely on the simple fact that the Highlands cannot feed all of its people. Bailie Jarvie—that shrewd but honorable businessman, always concerned with pounds, shillings and pence, yet not quite as indifferent as he pretends to pedigree, family history, and his distant relationship to Rob Roy—makes an admirable embodiment of the Lowland spirit. However, as David Craig observes, "The action in which Bailie Jarvie has to play a part breaks down into a series of adventures";[6] and, although Scott rouses our interest in this theme (the contrast), he fails to satisfy it.

There are some striking scenes, notably that at the inn at Aberfoil, which forms a most effective introduction to the primitive society of the Highlands; some amusing dialogue in the vernacular; a dashing heroine to fall in love with; and, after the first two hundred pages, an abundance of adventures and picturesque scenery. For the reader who asks no more than that the author make one thing happen after another, and so keep him turning the pages, these qualities may be enough. *Rob Roy* was a highly successful entertainment, but it can hardly be considered a serious work of art.

II Black Dwarf

The Black Dwarf (1816) and *A Legend of Montrose* (1819) may be briefly considered together but out of their chronological order; they are the shortest and, by general agreement, the weakest of the "Scotch Novels." *The Black Dwarf* offers the reader nothing new, except in its title character. The setting is the Border in 1707, during the threat of a Jacobite rising; but the Jacobite theme is not treated seriously. Perhaps the only novelty is Scott's satirical presentation of Jacobite motives as the conspirators gather and encourage themselves with liquor:

"Our commerce is destroyed," hallowed old John Rewcastle, a Jedburgh smuggler, from the lower end of the table.

"Our agriculture is ruined," said the Laird of Broken-girth-flow, a territory which, since the days of Adam, had borne nothing but ling and whortle-berries.

"Our religion is cut up, root and branch," said the pimple-nosed pastor of the Episcopal meeting-house at Kirkwhistle.

"We shall shortly neither dare shoot a deer nor kiss a wench without a certificate from the presbytery and kirk-treasurer," said Marischal Wells.

"Or make a brandy jeroboam in a frosty morning without license from a commissioner of the excise," said the smuggler.

"Or ride over the fell in a moonless night," said Westburnflat, "without asking leave of young Earnscliff or some Englified justice of the peace. Thae were gude days on the Border when there was neither peace nor justice heard of."

This selfish aspect of the movement undoubtedly existed and was probably quite as important as pure chivalry and honor. Scott seldom chose, however, to emphasize it, although in *Waverley* he clearly implied that Fergus Mac-Ivor is moved as much by ambition and vanity as by disinterested devotion to the Stuart cause. The gradual civilizing of the Border, hinted at in Westburnflat's speech quoted above, might have provided a unifying theme; instead, Scott makes it of only peripheral interest. Among the characters, Earnscliff and Isabel Ellieslaw are stock lovers; and old Ellieslaw is simply a heavy father. Hobbie Elliot and his family are presented with realism and charm, but Scott had done the same better with Dandie Dinmont in *Guy Mannering.* Although Westburnflat, the last Border outlaw, is an interesting conception, Scott fails to develop the potential of the character.

But the principal interest of the work depends on the Dwarf, in whom some critics, beginning with Lockhart, have discovered a quite uncharacteristic revelation of Scott's inner life—normally Scott was the most impersonal and objective of writers. *The Black Dwarf,* writes Lockhart melodramatically, "derives a singular interest from its delineation of the dark feelings so often connected with physical deformity; feelings which appear to have diffused their shadow over the whole genius of Byron—and which, but for this single picture, we should hardly have conceived ever to have passed through Scott's happier mind. All the bitter blasphemy of spirit which, from infancy to the tomb, swelled up in Byron . . . which sometimes perverted even his filial love into a sentiment of diabolical malignity; all this black and desolate train of reflections must have been encountered and deliberately subdued by the manly parent of the Black Dwarf." [7] And Lockhart's opinion is supported by a curious coincidence: on first reading *The Black Dwarf,* Byron's half-sister, Mrs. Leigh, was convinced that her brother had written it (it was published anonymously).

But this interpretation cannot be accepted. There is no evidence anywhere in Scott's letters or journals, not to mention his published writings, that he responded to his lameness with such Byronic bitterness. Even if he had, he was the last writer to reveal such intimate feelings to the public. It was not for Scott to exhibit to Europe and the world, as Matthew Arnold wrote of Byron, "the pageant of his bleeding heart." Perhaps the most convincing evidence of all can be found in the Dwarf's language. " 'Common humanity!' exclaimed the being, with a scornful laugh that sounded like a shriek, 'where got ye that catch-word—that noose for woodcocks—that common disguise for mantraps—that bait which the wretched idiot who swallows will soon find covers a hook with barbs ten times sharper than those you lay for the animals which you murder for your luxury!" Surely this is conventional rant, and the Dwarf himself is basically a stock type, one obviously influenced by the fashionable Byronism of the time.

Scott's own judgment of the work may be accepted: "not very original in its concoction, and lame and impotent in its conclusion." [8]

III   A Legend of Montrose

A Legend of Montrose is set entirely in the Scottish Highlands in 1644, and this setting in itself may account for the book's weakness. Both the time and the place are beyond Scott's imaginative reach. (Several of the novels contain Highland scenes, of course, but in no other does the action occur entirely within the Highlands.) The Earl of Montrose led a rising of the Highland clans against the Scottish government, which had supported the Parliamentary side in the English civil war. Montrose's rebellion, with its almost incredible series of victories against great odds and its sudden crushing defeat, might have provided a striking subject, but Scott largely ignores the historical events. His plot is concerned with a triangle involving the usual genteel hero and heroine and the Highlander Allan M'Aulay who believes himself to be gifted with the second sight. Interest derives (or is meant to derive) principally from Allan's prophecy that the hero, his rival and former friend, will be stabbed by a Highlander whose identity Allan cannot foretell. The stabbing occurs, but the hero recovers —the assailant is Allan himself.

Of the characters, Dugald Dalgetty, the Lowland soldier of fortune, may have attracted attention at least partly because he is the only figure in the novel to speak a vernacular Scots. The Gaelic of the Highlanders is rendered by a pseudopoetic diction strongly resembling the speech of a Cooper Indian (perhaps a literary influence could be traced here). One example will suffice: "'Kenneth,' said the old outlaw, 'hear the last words of the sire of thy father. A Saxon soldier and Allan of the Red Hand left this camp within these few hours, to travel to the country of Caberfae. Pursue them as the bloodhound pursues the hurt deer, swim the lake, climb the mountain, thread the forest, tarry not until you join them.'" In the tragedy of Allan M'Aulay, who believes himself gifted with the second sight and who foresees himself treacherously murdering a friend, Scott treats a subject similar to that of *Guy Mannering*, or at least of the beginning of *Guy Mannering*; but he is again unable to deal with it seriously, partly because, as in *Guy Mannering*, he seems unable to decide whether or not supposed supernatural powers should be accepted at face value or rationally explained as due either to coincidence or to a deranged imagination.

But, of course, one does not read to learn whether or not Allan's prophecies will be fulfilled; one reads to get more of Major Dalgetty. The character seems derived equally from Shakespeare's Fluellen (the military pedant) and from two seventeenth-century Scottish mercenaries, Colonel Robert Monro and Sir James Turner, whose memoirs Scott had read. To these sources may be added, as Buchan suggests,[9] a dash of Ben Jonson's Bobadil (and the *miles gloriosus* in general), of Smollet's Lismahago in *Humphrey Clinker*, and, perhaps, of Falstaff, in Dalgetty's devotion to food and drink. Certainly, the elements of which Dalgetty is composed are not original; but the product definitely is. Nothing could be more individual than the mixture of unscrupulousness, selfishness, vanity, pedantry, and religious cant displayed in his language:

I have heard enough since I came here to satisfy me that a cavalier of honour is free to take any part in this civil embroilment whilk he may find most convenient for his own peculiar. "Loyalty" is your password, my lord; "Liberty," roars another chield. . . . "The King," shouts one war-cry; "The Parliament," roars another; "Montrose for ever," cries Donald, waving his bonnet; "Argyle and Leven," cries a south-country Saunders. . . . "Fight for the bishops," says a priest, with his gown and rochet; "Stand stout for the Kirk," cries a minister, in a Geneva cap and band—good watchwords all—excellent watchwords. Whilk cause is the best I cannot say. But sure am I that I have fought knee-deep in blood many a day for one that was ten degrees worse than the worst of them all.

This speech not only characterizes Dalgetty, it satirizes all of the inspiring slogans, equally noble on either side, for which men kill. It is true that Dalgetty is a "flat" character, to use E. M. Forster's term, in that he does not develop or change. But the reader is quite satisfied to see how, like Falstaff, he extricates himself from every predicament. Although perhaps not the most original, he is certainly one of the richest of Scott's comic characters, and it might be said (if the paradox is permissible) that his humor provides the most serious interest of *A Legend of Montrose*.

CHAPTER 8

The Heart of Midlothian

*T*HE *Heart of Midlothian* (originally *Tales of My Landlord,
Second Series) was published in four volumes in July, 1818,
about six months after *Rob Roy*. Its instant and extraordinary success is indicated by a letter from Scott's friend Lady Louisa
Stuart: "I have not only read it myself, but am in a house where
everybody is tearing it out of each other's hands, and talking of
nothing else. . . . Had this very story been conducted by a common hand, Effie would have attracted all our concern and sympathy—Jeanie only cold approbation. Whereas Jeanie, without
youth, beauty, genius, warm passions, or any other novel-perfec-
tion, is here our object from beginning to end. This is 'enlisting the
affections in the cause of virtue' ten times more than ever Richardson did." [1]

The success of *Midlothian* has continued, and the majority of
Scott's critics have considered it his finest novel. Indeed, it has
been within the last ten years the subject of four or five critical
articles; no other Scott novel has received nearly as much attention. One reason for this preference is negative—the absence of
the conventional hero and heroine whom readers have always recognized as Scott's weakest characters. The novel really has no
hero, since George Staunton, Effie's seducer, is at least half a villain; and Reuben Butler, Jeanie's lover and later husband, plays a
minor role. Moreover, the heroine is for once drawn from the
lower classes, the social level at which Scott's creative power
worked most vigorously and freely. Lady Louisa's comment on
the moral value of the novel indicates another reason for its nineteenth-century popularity: a book containing both David and
Jeanie Deans would do much to overcome lingering scruples
about novel reading as a frivolous, morally suspect activity. Twentieth-century critics ordinarily do not care for moral improvement

in fiction, at least not in the direct sense; but they find that Jeanie's moral dilemma, whether or not to save her sister's life by a lie, gives the novel a seriousness lacking elsewhere in Scott.

I *The Narrative*

The story may be summarized briefly. After a rather tedious introductory chapter—Jedediah Cleishbotham and the whole machinery involved in the narrative frame of *Tales of My Landlord* are superfluous—the novel jumps back from the Scotland of 1818 to that of 1737. David Deans, a cowfeeder (dairy farmer) living near Edinburgh, has two daughters, Effie and Jeanie. Effie, the younger and more beautiful, is seduced by George Staunton, a dissipated young Englishman of wealth and good family who has become inextricably involved with criminal associates. Effie, whose baby mysteriously disappears, under a harsh law of the time is presumptively guilty of child-murder since she had communicated her pregnancy to no one and since the baby cannot be produced. Jeanie can save her life by declaring that Effie had told her of her condition; but when she refuses to lie, Effie is sentenced to death. Jeanie travels alone to London, gains the favor and help of the Duke of Argyle, has an interview with the queen, and obtains a pardon for her sister. Jeanie, her father, and Reuben Butler are befriended by Argyle and live out their lives prosperously and contentedly on his estate of Roseneath in the Highlands. Effie and Staunton are married; but Staunton is finally killed by his own son, now a Highland outlaw (father and son are unknown to each other), who then flees to America and joins an Indian tribe.

The Heart of Midlothian falls into four distinct sections. Chapters two to seven deal with the Porteous riot during which the Tolbooth prison is captured by a mob and the hated Captain Porteous is lynched; chapters eight through twenty-four are concerned primarily with the trial and condemnation of Effie and with Jeanie's moral quandary, but also present the background of the Deans family; chapters twenty-five through thirty-nine are concerned with Jeanie's journey to London and her efforts to win the pardon; chapters forty through fifty-two show Jeanie's marriage, her settlement at Roseneath, the marriage of Effie and George Staunton, and the death of Staunton. But the critical praise which the novel has received is based principally on the second part, seventeen chapters out of fifty-two. The first section, dealing with the Porteous riot, is a good historical reconstruction; but the episode is only tenuously connected with the central action: Staunton is supposed to have raised the riot in the hope of rescuing Effie from prison. Perhaps its relevance might best be defended by the argument that it effectively illustrates the temper of the time and the situation of Scotland.

Part three—the journey to London and the obtaining of the pardon—by general agreement shows a considerable falling off of interest. The principal difficulty seems to be that Jeanie is no longer a free agent; consequently, she is much less interesting. First she is kidnapped by outlaws; then rescued by a madwoman; and, when she arrives in London, her affairs are entirely managed by the Duke of Argyle, evidently a favorite hero of Scott. It is impossible to agree, however, with critics who feel that the novel's proper ending was with Effie's sentence. Jeanie, not Effie Deans, is the center of interest; and her journey to London is the inevitable consequence, given her boldness and determination, of her refusal to lie at Effie's trial. And what would our impression of Jeanie be if her sister had been hanged for the sake of her conscience?

Part four has been condemned as superfluous by nearly all critics. Only John Buchan has attempted a defense: "Scott was always social historian as well as novelist, and he wanted to show Scottish life passing into a mellower phase in which old unhappy things were forgotten. Artistically, too, the instinct was sound. The figures, who have danced so wildly at the bidding of fate, should find reward in a gentle, bright, leisurely old age. Even so Tolstoy rounded off his *War and Peace*." [2] But most readers find that their interest flags; and that the moral effect of the work is considerably weakened by Scott's obvious wish to make virtue more than its own reward and vice more than its own punishment.

In reality, Scott's motive for writing this epilogue seems to have been purely commercial. In November, 1817, he had contracted for an unwritten, unplanned, and even unthought of work to be published in four volumes; and he had used the royalty advance to pay off a large personal debt. Consequently, the fourth volume had to be written whether his story required it or not. In turn,

Scott's publisher, a contemporary reviewer suggested, "wished a fourth volume in the way of trade that he might, with more show of justice, charge the exorbitant price of £1 12s." [3]

II *Theme*

Recent critics have justified their preference for *The Heart of Midlothian* by finding in it a thematic significance which provides it with a degree of unity and seriousness not found in any other of the Waverley Novels. One critic, Robin Mayhead, begins his analysis with a full admission of Scott's normal artistic slackness: "Inconsistencies of plot and character, internal contradiction, anachronisms" seem not to have troubled Scott or his readers. "He is normally content to let the tale with its rather grey prose and its slack construction amble along as it pleases, quickening the pulse and tightening the grip only when the matter is of more than usual interest to him." [4] This looseness results from the lack of a central theme, or preoccupation, to give coherence to the work. However, *The Heart of Midlothian* is a novel "in which, if only for one-half of its length, Scott is sufficiently mastered by a theme to be inspired to a piece of almost entirely consistent artistic achievement." This theme the critic finds to be the question, "What does human justice amount to?" as exemplified in this law and in this case. [5] Unfortunately, the argument is supported by forced interpretations and by a good deal of critical oversubtlety.

The introductory chapter, which simply serves the purpose of introducing the supposed source of the story and of so "authenticating" it, is found to be an "obliquely ironic preface," presumably because of the rather flippant conversation of the two young lawyers who appear. As they talk, "Are these the men, we shall find ourselves asking, who guide the dispensers of human justice? . . . how essentially heartless they seem, how little more than a *profession* the Law is to them." But they are presented as thoroughly good-hearted young men, and there seems to be no reason in the novel itself that such a question should arise. Saddletree, Mayhead finds, "has the effect, in his long and overwhelming outpourings of legal jargon, of reducing the Law to nothing but an arid and absurd mechanism of phrases and abstractions, quite unconnected with the human beings it is supposed to govern." But Saddletree is a bore and a pedant of a kind very familiar in Scott's work. He serves the plot occasionally, but his primary function (hardly carried out) seems to be to provide comic relief.

The most serious defect of such an interpretation, however, is that the novel really contains no serious questioning either of the particular law or of the whole legal machine—nothing in fact but Mrs. Saddletree's half-humorous comment that "if the law makes murders, the law should be hanged for them; or if they wad hang a lawyer instead, the country wad find nae faut." Neither does the novel, directly or by implication, question the fact that Effie, who is guilty of nothing more than unchastity, can be saved from hanging only by an arbitrary exertion of royal authority. It is simply a given condition of the action, which both Jeanie and Scott take for granted.

Other critics have centered their attention on the religious atmosphere of the novel and found the unifying factor there. P. F. Fisher observes: "Unlike some of his contemporaries, Scott does not see God in the course of nature . . . but in a providential ordering of individual lives within the pattern of confirmed tradition." [6] Such a concept is certainly clearly illustrated, particularly in the later lives of the major characters. The critic adds: "It is evident through the remainder of the novel that any principle, however rigorously, and perhaps mistakenly, interpreted, is better than no principle. . . . This might be called the faith of the conservative romancer." David Deans's principles may at times be fantastic, but they provide an integrity of character, an emotional stability, and a sense of meaning in his life. Effie and Staunton demonstrate clearly enough, in their confused and turbulent lives, that good impulses cannot compensate for a lack of such a principle.

A slightly different significance has been discovered by David Craig, who suggests that "what underlies these chapters [nine to nineteen] and is brought out by almost every touch in them, is the moral and religious ethos produced by Presbyterianism." [7] Considerable justification can be found for this view, for in no other Waverley novel are the actions of the principal character so consistently controlled by religious belief. Even in *Old Mortality*, which deals with the revolt of the extreme Presbyterians against the government of Charles II, the hero, Morton, seems not to be influenced in the least by religious considerations. Jeanie's scruples, her refusal to lie, and her faith in a providential ordering of events, which gives her courage to undertake the journey to London and confidence that she will succeed, all spring from her religious faith. Her father, David Deans, is a kind of archetype of Scottish Presbyterianism (at least of the Cameronian variety) and of the sectarian spirit. Deans is a hair-splitter, a quibbler, a dogmatist who has perfect confidence in his own infallibility and in his unique ability to thread his way safely between "right-hand snares and extremes and left-hand wayslidings." "I am not a MacMillanite, or a Russelite, or a Hamiltonian, or a Harleyite, or a Howdenite," he declares; but he is a Deanite, a sect having one member, possibly two. "Though I will neither exalt myself nor pull down others, I wish every man and woman in this land had kept the true testimony, and the middle and straight path, as it were, on the ridge of a hill . . . as weel as Johnny Dodds of Farthing's Acre, and ae man mair that shall be nameless." This quotation clearly reveals his enormous spiritual pride, which is made explicit by his hearer, Bailie Middleburgh: "That is as much as to say, that Johnny Dodds of Farthing's Acre, and David Deans of St. Leonard's, constitute the only members of the true, real, unsophisticated Kirk of Scotland?"

Deans's conventional disclaimer is hardly convincing: "God forbid that I suld make sic a vain-glorious speech, when there are sae mony professing Christians!" This subtlety of characterization is not common in Scott. The same sureness and delicacy of touch is found in the implicit contrast between Deans's fantastic scruples about whether or not to recognize the existing government by allowing his daughter to testify in court and by Jeanie's facing of the fundamental moral issue of ends and means. Briefly, one might say that Jeanie represents the Presbyterian spirit purified of the harshness, intolerance, dogmatism, and concern with minutiae displayed by her father (just as Deans himself lacks the bloodthirstiness of the Covenanters in *Old Mortality*). It should be added that Deans possessed a natural eloquence and a basic dignity in spite of occasional absurdities.

But this sense of the "Presbyterian ethos" is not enough in itself to provide unity and coherence for more than a fraction of the novel. The basic, and fatal, structural flaws pointed out remain. One cannot, after all, separate the live parts of a novel from the dead; chapters eight through twenty-four cannot in themselves make a successful work of art. There are other, and obvious, weaknesses as well. It can be pointed out that Scott finally evades the moral issue, since Jeanie's decision to tell the truth does not, after all, cost her sister's life. Perhaps he should not be blamed severely, however; Shakespeare evaded a similar issue in *Measure for Measure*. More seriously, Scott never really renders Jeanie's actual process of decision. "O father, we are cruelly sted between God's laws and man's laws—what shall we do?" Jeanie exclaims; but, in a single paragraph of logical argument, Scott has her arrive at her decision. The sense of Jeanie's agony which the reader should have in order to acquit her of a callous and self-righteous concern for her own conscience at the expense of her sister's life is not given. "Has Jeanie an interesting conscience?" [8] an unsympathetic critic has asked; and the answer must be that she has not. It is not enough for Scott merely to *say* that "She remained in a state of the most agitating terror and uncertainty." It has already been pointed out that Jeanie's stature is reduced by the appearance of the Duke of Argyle as *deus ex machina*, and the moral impression of her actions is diminished still more by the very solid rewards—a trunkful of clothes, a house, comfortable positions for her husband and father—which she receives. Scott must have it both ways: Jeanie must tell the truth and still save Effie's life; she must receive the approval of her own conscience and material prosperity as well.

An excellent example of this tendency, incidentally, is found in Chapter fifty-one, when Scott evokes the pathetic fallacy, then dismisses it on rational grounds, then justifies it: "The dead and heavy closeness of the air, the huge piles of clouds which assembled in the western horizon, and glowed like a furnace under the influence of the setting sun—that awful stillness in which nature seems to expect the thunder-burst, as a condemned soldier waits for the platoon-fire which is to stretch him on the earth, all betokened a speedy storm. . . . 'There is something solemn in this delay of the storm,' said Sir George; 'it seems as if it suspended its peal till it solemnised some important event in the world below.'"

Butler's reply is that of eighteenth-century enlightenment: " 'What are we, that the laws of nature should correspond in their march with our ephemeral deeds or sufferings? The clouds will burst when surcharged with the electric fluid, whether a goat is falling at that instant from the cliffs of Arran, or a hero expiring on the field of battle he has won.' " Butler's answer shows that the author is a rational man who will not accept Staunton's superstition, but the description of the imminent storm is plainly meant to have the same effect on the reader that the sight has on Staunton —and Staunton's interpretation is supported by events.

What is evident here is a lack of seriousness or, in other terms, of an artistic conscience. This lack allowed Scott to add a fourth volume of pure padding, to include the outrageously caricatured Dumbiedykes (who really doesn't belong in this novel, he is so contrary to its prevailing tone), and to cheapen his effects even in the most vital section of the novel by such crude melodrama as Staunton's midnight interview with Jeanie. Instead of serious treatment of a complex moral problem, "we are given highwaymen and kidnapping and queens and colorful eccentrics." [9] There are naturally many incidental good things in *The Heart of Midlothian* which have not yet been mentioned—such minor characters as Ratcliffe and Sharpitlaw, some pleasant comedy as Jeanie records her naïve impressions of England, and snatches everywhere of Scots dialogue. But these qualities do not compensate for such basic defects. Another of the novel's recent critics has observed that it is Scott's best work because "Scott's own national, antiquarian and legal interests were called more constantly, more powerfully (but not, on the whole, more significantly) into play than elsewhere by the story of the peasant heroine who symbolises the national spirit of her race, rank and time." [10] And this characteristic seems to be the most that can justifiably be claimed for the work.

In the long run, the greatest significance of *The Heart of Midlothian* probably does not lie in its artistic achievement, but in its contribution to the development of the English novel. It is difficult for the modern reader to recognize the novelty of such a heroine as Jeanie Deans, but never before her had a person of her social class been the protagonist of a long, serious novel. Never had such a character been treated with so much understanding and sympathy and so little condescension, without either sentimentalization or caricature. *The Heart of Midlothian* helped to democratize the novel; it opened for the serious novelist a new range of subject matter and character.

CHAPTER 9

The Waverley Novels—
Their Place in Literature

WITH *The Bride of Lammermoor* and with *A Legend of Montrose,* published together in 1819, the series of novels set in the Scotland of the preceding hundred and fifty years comes to an end—and so also does Scott's significant contribution to the English novel. Only when Scott returned to his favorite scene and period, as in *Redgauntlet* and the short story, "The Two Drovers," did his work reach its former level. The decline was recognized by the more discriminating readers—the principal journals either stopped reviewing the novels entirely or reviewed them two or three at a time rather than individually—but the public demand continued. And Scott, urged on by his publishers and by his ever increasing need of money, literally worked himself to death to satisfy it.

I *Novelty of Time, Place*

Scott's great fear was of wearing out his public, and his principal artistic aim in this last period seems to have been to attain novelty, usually by the choice of a previously unexploited setting or period. In *Ivanhoe* (1819) Scott turned to the England of Richard Coeur de Lion, King John, and Robin Hood and achieved his greatest popular success as English readers responded with patriotic enthusiasm to this treatment of their own history. Scott was attracted to the period by the possibilities of developing a striking contrast between Norman and Saxon: "It seemed to the Author" he explains in his introduction, "that the existence of the two races in the same country, the vanquished distinguished by their plain, homely, blunt manners, and the free spirit infused by their ancient institutions and laws; the victors, by the high spirit of military fame, personal adventure, and whatever could distinguish them as the flower of chivalry, might . . . interest the reader by the contrast, if the Author should not fail on his part." Whether such a contrast actually existed in the England of the early thirteenth century is very doubtful; but what is more damaging to *Ivanhoe* as a work of art is that Scott develops it superficially; he gives his subject none of the rich significance with which he had endowed the opposition of Highlands and Lowlands.

Scott's imagination worked most freely and powerfully when dealing with Scottish characters, usually though not always of the lower classes, who speak their native vernacular. In *Ivanhoe*, of course, there could be no such characters or speech. Instead, Scott employs "tushery"—that is, a heavily formal English archaized by medieval or pseudomedieval terms and by occasional inverted word order: " 'So much the better,' said Front-de-Boeuf, 'that he comes here to give me my revenge. Some hilding fellow he must be, who dared not stay to assert his claim to the tourney prize which chance had assigned him. I should in vain have sought for him where knights and nobles seek their foes, and right glad am I he hath here shown himself among yon villain yeomanry.' " Scott employs an interesting technical device when he chooses to present the attack on Torquilstone Castle through Rebecca's description rather than by direct narration, and the novel approaches serious significance in the debate between Rebecca and the wounded Ivanhoe on the meaning of honor; but Grierson's summary seems accurate: Scott "had written what is mainly a good story of adventure for boys." [1] "*Was* a good adventure story for boys," might be a more accurate description, since *Ivanhoe* is now usually read under compulsion.

The Monastery and *The Abbot* (1820) are set in the Scotland of Queen Mary, a period beyond Scott's imaginative grasp. His difficulty is most clearly shown in the fantastic linguistic confusion of the two novels; his characters speak in Euphuism, "tushery," standard English, and vernacular Scots. *The Monastery* contains Scott's most extended use of the supernatural in the White Lady of Avenel—an attempt which fails from the flat literalness of the presentation. *Kenilworth* (1821) is a novel of the Elizabethan Age with a tragic subject—the murder of Amy Robsart, secret wife of Queen Elizabeth's favorite, the Earl of Leicester—but the tragedy is smothered under pageantry and antiquarianism. *The Fortunes of Nigel* (1822) is notable principally for its much admired pre-

sentation of James I. Coleridge's comment, "Burlesque, not character . . . Sir Walter Scott copies Shakespeare's Holofernes and
calls him King James," [2] contains some truth; but, on the whole,
Scott realizes for the reader "the wisest fool in Christendom." The
fact that James is allowed to speak his native Scots would in itself
distinguish him in the novel. *The Pirate* (1821), set in the Ork-
neys in the early eighteenth century and *Peveril of the Peak*
(1823), dealing with the Popish Plot during the reign of Charles
II, attracted little attention even in their own time, and Scott's last
great popular success came with *Quentin Durward* in 1823. The
center of interest is the contrast between Louis XI and Charles the
Bold, Duke of Burgundy—both selfish, unscrupulous and ambitious. Charles—violent, impetuous, and stupid—loves pageantry
and war; Louis—miserly, cautious, controlled, farsighted, indifferent to fame and reputation—concentrates on the reality of power.
The two figures represent the past and the future—and the
worst of each, one might add. The entire novel really exists for the
sake of its climactic scene, the long-delayed confrontation of
Louis and Charles. For once Scott prepared carefully for a scene
and then developed all its potentialities. *Quentin Durward* greatly
widened Scott's European, particularly his French, reputation and
influence.

St. Ronan's Well (1824) is Scott's closest approach to contemporary realism, but the book is seriously injured by his concession
to the prudery of his printer, James Ballantyne, who objected to
the seduction of the aristocratic heroine, even though it was supposed to have occurred before the beginning of the story. Scott,
who recognized the absurdity of the complaint, remarked: "You
would never have quarrelled with it had the thing happened to a
girl in gingham:—the silk petticoat can make little difference." [3]
Nevertheless, he "consented to cancel and rewrite about twenty-
four pages, which was enough to obliterate, to a certain extent,
the dreaded scandal—and in a similar degree, as he always per-
sisted, to perplex and weaken the course of his narrative, and the
dark effect of its catastrophe." [4]

Redgauntlet (1825) requires no further criticism. Little needs
to be said about the remaining works. *Woodstock* (1826), which
Buchan unaccountably called the best-written of all the novels,
deals with the escape of Charles II after the battle of Worcester.

It attempts to exploit a Cavalier-Roundhead contrast, but so conventionally and superficially as to lack any serious interest; and its often-admired portrait of Cromwell seems exaggerated and melodramatic. Buchan's comment on this characterization that "if he is not altogether the real man, he is nearer the historical truth than any picture of him before Carlyle"[5] may be justified; but the historical accuracy of the description cannot, in itself, increase the *literary* interest of *Woodstock* in the least.

The Talisman (1825) was once admired for its portrayal of Saladin and Richard Coeur de Lion, but its melodramatics can hardly be taken seriously. *The Fair Maid of Perth* (1828), set in medieval Scotland, contains the most vigorous of all Scott's heroes in Henry Wynd, an energetic fighter and lover. *Anne of Geierstein* (1829) is a rather dull historical sequel to *Quentin Durward*. *Castle Dangerous* and *Count Robert of Paris* (1832) did not even reach the level of successful entertainments and reveal the effects of Scott's stroke. The short story, "The Two Drovers" (1827) has more vitality than anything else from these years. In it Scott developed for the last time the familiar Highland-Lowland (in this case England, but the significance remains the same) contrast, each side being represented by one of the drovers of the title. The action develops from their conflicting legal and ethical standards, and from the difference in "manners" of their societies; and, for once, events are allowed to reach their natural tragic conclusion.

The novels from 1819 to 1825 suffer from the pressure under which they were composed (three a year in 1820 and 1822) as Scott tried to cope with his mounting expenses and as his publishers egged him on in order to capitalize as quickly as possible on his declining popularity. His work after 1826 is that of a worn-out man who was trying desperately to retain his fading popularity by novelty of scene or period—medieval Switzerland, Syria, and Palestine during the Crusades, the eleventh-century Byzantine Empire (*Count Robert*), even the almost contemporary India of Hyder Ali and Tippoo Sahib (*The Surgeon's Daughter*). Failing health, overwork, and exhaustion, as well as anxiety over his debts and worry over political developments (this was the stormy period of Catholic Emancipation and the first Reform Bill)—all contributed to the decline. Finally, it appears that with *Redgauntlet*

Scott had exhausted his true subject matter; he had written himself out, but refused to admit it.

II *Qualities of the Novels*

Surveying the Waverley Novels as a whole, one is struck by a purely negative quality: the lack of development shown in some thirty novels written over a period of about sixteen years. One could say without exaggeration that Keats developed more in six months than Scott did in sixteen years. It is not surprising that a writer's first novel should contain the germ of everything he is later to achieve, but *Waverley* contains the achievement as well. There is no sign of the steadily increasing psychological penetration, mastery of technique, and complexity of moral vision which the work of Jane Austen, for example, displays. Instead, after the first half dozen "Scotch novels" a steady decline sets in and Scott's work becomes increasingly superficial and repetitious; moreover, the formula on which his novels were constructed becomes more and more obvious. Part of the explanation no doubt lies in Scott's maturity when he began his career as a novelist, but, after all, intellectual and emotional development need not stop when a writer passes forty—too many examples prove the opposite. The experiences of childhood and youth probably are the most significant for most writers—indeed, for most human beings; but for Scott, as for Mark Twain, they formed his entire literary capital. When he had used up that capital, he had nothing more to say. He apparently was unable to convert his adult experience into material for fiction or to deal, in his novels, with the Scotland in which he lived.

It is not surprising, then, that Scott's characters tend to repeat themselves. "How uniformly Scott fails in his attempt at imaginative characters!" Coleridge exclaimed. "They are all alike from Meg Merrilies to Norna." [6] Certainly Meg Merrilies, Madge Wildfire, Norna of the Fitful Head are to a considerable degree mechanical and predictable figures. (This characteristic was also foreshadowed in *Waverley*; Davie Gellatly in that novel is simply a male variant of the type.) The bores and pedants too are much alike from beginning to end. Then there is what might be called "the Dandie Dinmont type"—the rough, honest, kindhearted farmer—and the shrewd, sometimes rascally servant who is contrasted with his impractical and "romantic" master, of which the best examples are Cuddie Headrigg in *Old Mortality* and Andrew Fairservice in *Rob Roy*. But the most striking of such repetitions is the sameness of the heroes and heroines in all of the novels—with only two partial exceptions: *The Heart of Midlothian,* in which the stock heroine does not appear at all and the stock hero (Reuben Butler) has a fortunately minor role; and *The Fair Maid of Perth* in which the hero, Henry Wynd, for once is drawn from the middle class, instead of the aristocracy, and displays a bourgeois vigor lacking in his counterparts.

In summary, readers and critics have always found the official heroes and heroines to be the least satisfactory characters of the Waverley Novels. From the vagueness with which they are described, it seems clear that Scott had never really imagined them; indeed, any pair of them would do almost equally well in any novel. The descriptions in *The Antiquary* could apply to them all: the hero is "a young man of genteel appearance" and the heroine is of "tall and elegant figure" (alternatively, she sometimes possesses a "fairy form"). The heroine is always blonde, with only one striking exception, Diana Vernon in *Rob Roy;* and Scott's formula for Rowena in *Ivanhoe* would apply to them all: "Her disposition was naturally that which physiognomists consider as proper to fair complexions—mild, timid, and gentle."

Scott's heroines, however, generally have only a minor part in the action; as a result, criticism has centered on the hero. He is essentially passive, "a thing never acting but perpetually acted upon," as Scott himself observed in *The Fortunes of Nigel*. The typical hero, like Lovel in *The Antiquary*, "asks nothing of society but the privilege of walking innoxiously through the path of life, without jostling others, or permitting myself to be jostled." Adolphus, in his *Letters to Richard Heber* (1822), was perhaps the first critic to consider this weakness of the hero at length. "It has frequently been noticed as a fault," writes Adolphus, "that the hero . . . is not sufficiently important, and fails to maintain his legitimate pre-eminence above the other characters. One circumstance very common . . . and highly disadvantageous to the principal personage, is, that during a great part of the story, he is made the blind or involuntary instrument of another's purposes, the attendant on another's will, and the sport of events over which he exercises no control" *[sic]* Thus the character of Frank Osbaldistone lacks the "commanding interest which should surround the first personage of a novel" because he is constantly "played upon as a dupe, disposed of as a captive, tutored as a novice." Adolphus also notes that "It is also the misfortune of many heroes in these works to be constantly thrown into shade by some more prominent character" [7] as Waverley is by Fergus Mac-Ivor, Frank Osbaldistone by Rob Roy, and Ivanhoe by King Richard.

A recent critic has pointed out the curious fact that, with only one or two exceptions, the Scott hero never kills anyone.[8] Certainly, it is a surprising fact when one considers that the heroes are gentlemen, necessarily accustomed to the use of weapons and ready to defend their honor, and that the action of many of the novels occurs in times or places characterized by violence, lawlessness, or civil war. Closely related to this subordination of the hero is the fact that he is often absent, or only a spectator, at some crucial scene; thus, Waverley "sinks into absolute insignificance, by sustaining only the part of a common spectator in the highly tragic scene of Mac-Ivor's and Evan Dhu's condemnation." [9]

A similar example occurs in *Old Mortality* when Morton, already secure of his pardon, watches the trial and torture of the Covenanters after their defeat at Bothwell Bridge. Again, the hero sometimes disappears from the novel for long periods, like Ivanhoe or Lovel in *The Antiquary*. The same comment holds true for the narrative poems. In *The Lady of the Lake*, Malcolm Graeme, the official hero, "continues in retirement till we hardly wish for his return," [10] as Adolphus remarks. It should be added that the passivity of the hero is mental as well as physical. At times he is supposed to suffer, but one has only Scott's bare statement to this effect, which is hardly convincing; the hero may be supposed to have struggles of conscience, but these internal conflicts are never presented.

Frequently contrasted with the passive, official hero is a character who may be called the "dark hero" [11]—Fergus Mac-Ivor, Rob Roy, Redgauntlet, Cleveland the Pirate, and George Staunton, among others, in the novels; Marmion, Bertram (in *Rokeby*), and Roderick Dhu in the poems. A contemporary reviewer noted that Scott's novels usually contained both "a virtuous passive hero, who is to marry the heroine" and "a fierce active hero, who is to die a violent death, generally by hanging or shooting." [12] This character is a mixture of good and evil; he lives by passion, impulse, and desire rather than by adherence to a rigid moral code. He acts and feels; naturally enough, he is usually the center of interest whenever he appears on the scene. The type is strongly Byronic in many respects, but represents an independent development by Scott; indeed, Marmion might be called a Byronic hero before Byron. A "dark heroine" may also be found in several of the novels. One thinks of Rowena, of Minna Troil in *The Pirate*, and Flora Mac-Ivor. This heroine is often more voluptuous in figure than the blonde heroine, and she always possesses a forcefulness, emotional intensity, and often a wit and intellectual capacity, which are quite lacking in the official heroine. Such characters apparently seemed morally ambiguous to Scott and appeared to threaten the established code (based on self-denial and restraint) and so to threaten the existence of society itself. Consequently, as has been noted, the dark heroes never outlive the novels in which they appear; the dark heroines, if permitted to live, are usually dispatched to a convent or to a state of lifelong spinsterhood.

Scott himself was quite aware of the deficiencies of his heroes; in fact, in his review of his own novels in the *Quarterly Review* he cited this weakness as one of the two main faults of the novels (the other being faulty construction of plot). Scott attempted to explain this characteristic passivity by the fact that his heroes were usually supposed to be strangers to Scotland, a fact which allowed the author to "enter into minute details, which are addressed to the reader through the medium of the hero," thus aiding the author's portrayal of manners. But Scott recognized that "if he [the author] gains this advantage, it is by sacrificing the character of the hero. No one can be interesting to the reader who is not, himself, a prime agent in the scene." [13] The explanation sounds suspiciously like a rationalization, and in any case will not hold for most of the Waverley Novels.

A few critics have attempted philosophic or esthetic justifications of the passive hero. Georg Lukacs explains, obviously with such novels as *Waverley* and *Old Mortality* in mind, that Scott chose as protagonist a figure who "may, through character and fortune, enter into human contact with both sides." [14] and so must not be a fanatical partisan of either extreme. But such an explanation is irrelevant to many of the Waverley Novels—*Guy Mannering* or *The Antiquary,* for example—which do not present violently contending parties but deal exclusively with private affairs. David Daiches combines a similar view of the function of the hero with Scott's own explanation that he is primarily an observer: "To censure Scott for the woodenness of his heroes . . . is to misunderstand their function. They are not heroes in the ordinary sense, but symbolic observers." [15] Such characters cannot "step out of their symbolic role in order to act freely and provide that sense of abundant life which is so essential to a good novel."

But surely a literary symbol, whether a character, object, or event, must be concrete—must appear real and convincing—to have effect. It must not be distinguished from the rest of the novel only by its vagueness or abstractness. This essential sense of life, Daiches continues, "is therefore achieved by the minor characters (and here again the comparison with Shakespeare suggests itself)." [16] One wonders what Shakespearean plays Daiches could have had in mind. When one thinks of the major plays, one thinks first of their central characters—of Hamlet rather than of Polonius. The Shakespearean comparison here seems as inappropriate as it generally does for Scott; as usual, it points up Scott's deficiencies all the more sharply.

Hazlitt, in an essay on "The Heroes of Romance," suggested that "a candidate for the highest favor of the public . . . must really have nothing in him to please or give offence." His character will be bland and wholesome marked only by a few good qualities, "which everyone may be supposed to improve upon and fill up according to his or her inclination." The hero is, inevitably, "a sort of blank left open to the imagination." Such an explanation seems to fit Scott's thoroughgoing commercialism. Hazlitt no doubt would have agreed with Scott's friend Lady Louisa Stuart that "the hero and the heroine are the people one cares least about. But provided one does care enough about somebody, it is all one to me." [17]

But such genial tolerance will hardly excuse Scott. If almost every reader is merely bored by the hero's personal affairs, by his speeches, by his love for the heroine, then there is a vacuum at the center of each novel which no amount of peripheral action or character can fill. It is doubtful too if the minor characters really benefit from the dullness of the major ones. Such figures as Meg Merrilies and Wandering Willie "are none of them central to the drama of the novel. They wander around the main life, turning up when needed to pass off coincidences and surprises." They are "vehicles for the author's 'good Scots' and his miscellaneous lore. Beside them, the official heroes and heroines shrink into puppets; but neither can such vehicles of idiom, lore, and 'character' get the status as human beings which they would if they could enter into relationships which affected the main course of the drama." [18]

Much of the effect, or lack of it, produced by the hero and heroine depends upon the language they speak, upon its extreme formality or "genteel" quality. Theirs is an abstract, polysyllabic, somewhat Latinate vocabulary and also a rather elaborate syntax. Examples have already been given (they can be found in abundance in every Scott novel), but one more may be cited from one of Scott's least known works, *Castle Dangerous* (1831). The heroine is desperately trying to interrupt a combat between two knights: "Think that this is Palm Sunday, and will you defile with blood such a peculiar festival of Christianity? Intermit your feud at least so far as to pass to the nearest church, bearing with you branches, not in the ostentatious mode of earthly conquerors, but as rendering due homage to the rulers of the blessed Church, and the institutions of our holy religion." The polysyllabic vocabulary is extremely marked, and one notices also the length of the second sentence. Such sentences are characteristic of Scott. Although the long sentence in itself cannot be considered a fault in dialogue— consider Faulkner or the later James—it should serve as a recognizable function, express what could not be expressed as well otherwise or help to characterize the speaker. None of these functions is fulfilled by the long sentences in a Scott novel. The length makes possible considerable elaboration of syntax and frequent pauses, sometimes delaying the completion of meaning and sometimes leading to repetitiousness and padding. In the example cited, the meaning is completed at the end of the opening independent clause, which is followed by a lengthy and unnecessary series of modifiers. In vocabulary, one frequently notices a curious inexactness of usage, which makes up a good part of the "slovenliness" of which contemporary reviewers regularly complained. Thus, from *The Antiquary*: " 'Were I compelled to decompose [*sic!*] the motives of my worthy friend."

This jargon is not entirely reserved for upper class characters; it is often extended, unhappily, to those of a lower level, like the gypsy Hayraddin Maugrabin, Quentin Durward's guide. "Where, then, is your boasted freedom?" asks Quentin, and Hayraddin replies: "In my thoughts, which no chains can bind; while yours, even when your limbs are free, remain fettered by your laws and your superstitions, your dreams of local attachment, and your fantastic visions of civil policy . . . ." Coleridge's comment on the passage seems fully justified: "Characterless or anti-characteristic as Scott's dialogues too commonly are, this is ultra-improbable, superlatively inappropriate." [19] Probably well-bred conversation in the early nineteenth century was more formal and ceremonious than it is today, but it could never have approached the style of such passages. Nor can Scott's dialogue be explained on the ground of literary convention; Jane Austen's characters do not speak like this, and neither do those of Fielding or Smollett.

Scott's narrative prose displays the same qualities, although less strikingly. It, too, is pretentious and diffuse, effectively "distancing" the action described, whether or not such distancing serves any esthetic function. Incidentally, since Scott's novels deal with physical action to so great an extent, it is surprising how ineffective his style is for presenting such material. One might consider, for example, the death of Brian Bois-Guilbert in *Ivanhoe*: "The trumpet sounded, and the knights charged each other in full career. The wearied horse of Ivanhoe and its no less exhausted rider, went down, as all had expected, before the well-aimed lance and vigorous steed of the Templar. This issue of the combat all had foreseen; but although the spear of Ivanhoe did but, in comparison, touch the shield of Bois-Guilbert, that champion, to the astonishment of all who beheld it, reeled in his saddle, lost his stirrups, and fell in the lists." One notes the vagueness of Ivanhoe's fall—he and his horse simply "went down." No more colorless verb could be found. And the passage is wordy; for example, the first clause of the third sentence is mere repetition, completely superfluous. The passage is wordy, yet at the same time too brief; the details which would enable the reader to *see* are simply not there. If he is to imagine the scene fully, he must really create it for himself. Apparently Scott's readers were so willing to do so, that they never noticed that the author had not performed his function.

Some critics, it is true, seem to believe that a novelist's style does not really matter. Yet a novel, after all, is made of words; and effectiveness depends on the manner in which the author arranges words. Style does matter in the Waverley Novels: the narrative style delays the communication of meaning and prevents the close involvement of the reader since the English dialogue too often prevents him from believing seriously in the emotions the characters are represented as feeling or in the characters themselves. Passion of any kind could never conceivably be expressed in such a style.

Apologizing for Scott's prose, Tillyard admits that pomposity and long-windedness are faults "to which all of Scott's novels are prone, and which, being occasional and inorganic, we are justified in passing over lightly"—just as Scott's contemporary reviewers did. Such an opinion will hardly stand analysis; faults which occur in every novel cannot be dismissed as "occasional"; and, as for "inorganic," it would be hard to imagine what could be more organic to a novel than its prose.[20] Virginia Woolf has provided a more radical defense. Admitting Scott's excessive Latinisms, his cliches, and his "poetic diction," she continues that, in context, "it is difficult either to notice or condemn them . . . they fulfill their purpose and merge perfectly in their surroundings. Great novelists who are going to fill seventy volumes write after all in pages, not in sentences, and have at their command, and know when to use, a dozen . . . styles . . . These slips and slovenlinesses serve as relaxations." [21] Relaxations for the writer, perhaps, but not for the reader! In spite of this dictum, it seems clear that pages are composed of sentences; and, if the sentences are ineffective, the pages can hardly succeed.

It has been stated before, and must now be repeated, that the Waverley Novels have two (not a dozen, as Virginia Woolf claims) styles, an English and a Scottish. The Scottish style occurs principally in dialogue, in the speech of lower- and middle-class characters and of upper-class ones who are treated humorously, such as Baron Bradwardine or James I. Scott uses it only once for

extended narrative, in "Wandering Willie's Tale" in *Redgauntlet*.
Examples enough have been quoted to suggest the wit, the liveli-
ness, the freshness of imagery, the rhythm, and the emotional intensity of this second style. Scott's predicament was that of Burns,
who complained "These English songs gravel me to death. I have
not the command of the language that I have of my native tongue
. . . I think my ideas are more barren in English than in Scottish." [22] When writing in stiff and conventional English, Burns was
simply a minor eighteenth-century versifier.

The linguistic situation Scott faced was entirely different from
that confronted by any English novelist, even a regionalist like
Thomas Hardy. Scots possessed a long, distinctive literary tradition and was still the generally spoken language of the country;
but broad Scots, at least, was beginning to disappear from the
speech of the educated. The declining prestige of the vernacular
was recognized and recorded by Scott himself in a letter of 1822:
"Scotch was a language which we have heard spoken by the
learned & the wise & witty . . . and which had not a trace of vulgarity in it, but on the contrary sounded rather graceful and genteel . . . it was different from the English as the Venetian from
Tuscan dialect of Italy, but it never ocurd [sic] to anyone that
the Scotish [sic] any more than the Venetian was more vulgar.
. . . But that is all gone."

Since the union of Scotland and England in 1707, and perhaps
even earlier, Scots had gone out of use as a medium of serious
prose. Except in a few popular chapbooks, its literary use throughout the eighteenth century was confined to poetry—primarily, of
course, the poetry of Burns. In the second half of the century,
with Hume, Robertson, Adam Smith, Lord Kames and others, Edinburgh produced a brilliant intellectual life. But, while these men
spoke Scots, they wrote standard English and carefully avoided
"Scotticisms." The Scottish writer was forced to use a "foreign language, which the English is to us," with all the difficulties it en-
tailed, Carlyle observed in his *Autobiography*. Some of these difficulties were described by Scott's friend, John Leyden. The Scots-
man of the upper classes was "prohibited, by the imputation of
vulgarity, from using the common language of the country, in
which he expresses himself with most ease and vivacity, and,
clothed in which, his earliest and most distinct impressions always

arise to his mind. He uses a species of translation, which checks the versatility of fancy, and restrains the genuine and spontaneous glow of his conceptions." [23] (It might be added that the stiffness of the passage itself illustrates Leyden's thesis.)

The necessity of making such a "species of translation" might almost fatally handicap the imaginative writer (Conrads and Nabokovs are extremely scarce), but would affect the philosopher or historian much less seriously. Thus it is not surprising that eighteenth-century Scotland was capable of first-class work in philosophy, psychology, and other intellectual fields, but that its principal achievement in "polite literature" (a category excluding Burns) was John Home's mediocre tragedy *Douglas* (1756). The Scottish writer has continued to be subject to this difficulty; one can see such a split between the two styles in Stevenson, although his English is certainly a great deal easier and more idiomatic than Scott's. In the twentieth century Scottish poets have created a literary language, "Lallans," out of the vernacular. No doubt the problem will persist until Scots is as completely replaced by standard English as Gaelic has been in Ireland (artificial revivals are not likely to have lasting success in either case).

One natural consequence of the linguistic situation was an extreme self-consciousness and consequent hyper-correctness and formality of style. "When an easy, idiomatical phrase occurs we dare not adopt it," wrote another of Scott's contemporaries. "We handle English, as a person who cannot fence handles a sword; continually afraid of hurting themselves with it . . . or making some awkward motion that shall betray our ignorance." [24] Such an explanation would account for the nature of Scott's English dialogue. Writing in Scots, or even a lightly Scotticized English like the language of "Wandering Willie's Tale," freed him from these inhibitions, from the paralyzing need to be "genteel" and correct. For the most part, however, he could use the vernacular only in dialogue; his own gentility and the fear of "imputation of vulgarity" and the requirements of his English audience alike ruled it out as a narrative medium. Scott's comment on Rob Roy's manner of speaking English perfectly characterizes his own style: he had the "slow, pedantic mode of expression, arising from a desire to avoid peculiarities of idiom or dialect."

Scott's English readers occasionally grumbled, when reading the earlier novels, about the need of a glossary to cope with the dialect, and one review attacked the "dark dialect of Anglified Erse" which many of his characters spoke, but the difficulties presented certainly did not interfere with his English popularity. Nevertheless, it seems likely that only a Scot can fully appreciate the earlier novels. Other readers may look up definitions of unfamiliar words in a glossary or in a dialect dictionary, but such definitions do not help them, as the *Edinburgh Review* observed, to "know their value, as expressive of certain feelings and humours in the speakers to whom they are native." [25]

Enough has been said already about Scott's methods of composition to suggest the weaknesses which would inevitably result. The novels were never planned and never revised; each chapter was sent to the printer as soon as its first draft was finished. Such a method naturally produces verbosity—a characteristic of Scott's—and the tendency was reinforced by the commercial necessity of filling three or four volumes whether the subject justified such length or not. Carlyle's acid comment on Lockhart's biography of Scott applies with equal aptness to the Waverley Novels: "Seven volumes sell so much dearer than one; are so much easier to write"; and one can hardly help agreeing with Carlyle's addition: "There is a great discovery still to be made in Literature, that of paying literary men by the quantity they *do not* write." [26]

Inevitably, too, there is in Scott's novels a tendency toward repetition and self-plagiarism. Scott's fondness for the striking contrast of cultures has been noted; but, whereas such a contrast often provides the most serious interest in the earlier novels, it later becomes a cliché, a device to be exploited for picturesque effects and for a superficial novelty. Scott's tendency to repeat himself in his characters has been discussed; the same repetitiousness exists in his plots. In 1822, the *Quarterly Review,* in discussing *The Fortunes of Nigel,* neatly summarized the typical plot of the Waverley Novels: "The poor passive hero is buffeted about in the usual manner, involved, as usual, in the chicaneries of civil process, and exposed to the danger of a criminal execution, and rewarded by the hand of the heroine, such as she is, and the redemption of the mortgage on the family estate." Usually the hero's social status is threatened and his honor and/or loyalty cast in doubt by suspicious circumstances until he finally demonstrates that he is a thoroughly respectable and conventional member of society.

As a maker of plots, Scott is not only repetitive but careless and awkward. His difficulties with beginnings and endings—the first often intolerably slow, the last huddled and perfunctory—are obvious. David Daiches' comment on *Redgauntlet* applies equally to most of the novels. *Redgauntlet*'s greatest weakness, Daiches remarks, is that Scott "uses the conventional plot patterns available to him to provide the external structure of his story, and these plot patterns are really quite unsuitable to the kind of exploration between tradition and progress which Scott is carrying out." [27] They not only are unsuitable; they frequently conflict with the serious theme. Scott was fond of quoting the satirical remark of Bayes in *The Rehearsal* that the plot exists in order to bring fine things in, and his own plots often seem to be merely devices for bringing in, awkwardly and improbably, the situations, scenes, and characters which he wished to present. Scott never developed a suitable form for his novels.

The primary interest of a Scott novel, however, depends on its scenes rather than on its plot; and Scott was constantly praised by contemporary reviewers, in surprisingly Jamesian terms, for his "dramatic merit," for his avoidance of the "common language of narrative," and for placing the reader "in the situation of the audience at a theater, who are compelled to gather the meaning of the scene from what the dramatis personae say to each other and not from any explanation addressed immediately to themselves" and so "think of the personages of the novel and not of the writer." [28] Other writers had already done the same (Jane Austen much more consistently and effectively), and Scott frequently intrudes himself into his narration, often quite unnecessarily; but the praise does contain truth.

The strength of a Scott novel lies in its parts rather than in the whole, in its minor characters, and in striking, isolated scenes. Scott's carelessness and unconcern about esthetic problems repeatedly damage the novels. He is constantly ready to digress. Thus in *Ivanhoe*, with Cedric and his party prisoners in Torquilstone Castle, with Isaac of York threatened with torture and the two heroines with rape, Scott breaks off his narration of Bracy's "courtship" of Rowena and recounts for a page and a half the cruelty and vices of the Norman nobility. Too often scenes lose much of their proper effect because of lack of preparation, and often the expected and essential scene is not presented at all.

Many of Scott's contemporaries seemed to feel that unity and coherence were unimportant, if only the novelist told a good story. Thus the *Edinburgh Review* in a comment about *The Fortunes of Nigel* pointed out that the hero's "own scanty part . . . is performed in the vicinity of a number of other separate transactions," which were all thrown into a single work. "We should not care very much," the reviewer continued, "if this only destroyed the unity of the piece—but it sensibly weakens its interest, and reduces it from the rank of a comprehensive and engaging narrative, in which every event gives and receives importance from its connexion with the rest, to that of a mere collection of sketches relating to the same periods." [29] With a curious naïveté, the reviewer quite unintentionally demonstrates conclusively that unity creates interest and so is not merely an irrelevant "artistic" consideration.

Scott was a historical novelist—the statement seems fatuously obvious; but it must be made. Only three of the entire series of Waverley Novels avoid this classification: *St. Ronan's Well,* which was immediately contemporary in its setting; *Guy Mannering;* and *The Antiquary.* Certainly a genre which has produced *War and Peace* cannot be despised, yet the historical novel has attracted little attention from serious critics and scholars in recent years. (The principal exception is the Hungarian Marxist, Georg Lukacs; the historical novel has a strong appeal for Marxist critics.) It has been pointed out that Scott was virtually the inventor of the form; for, although Gothic novels might have medieval settings, they were certainly not historical in any sense. Lukacs suggests, quite plausibly, that the development of the historical novel at this particular period was influenced by the historical events of the age, that the enormous political upheavals of the revolutionary and Napoleonic period must have indicated very powerfully the direct effect of history upon individual lives.

The closest literary analogues to Scott's novels were the history plays of Shakespeare, and Scott may very well have learned a good deal from them, particularly from Shakespeare's readiness to mingle the humorous with the serious or tragic—to include Bardolph, Pistol, and Fluellen in the same play as the heroic Henry V. Shakespeare's attention is more centered on the major historical figures, however; in his earlier novels, at least, Scott treated such personages with a good deal of discretion by usually introducing them only briefly and by never allowing them to play central roles in the action. Unlike Shakespeare's histories, a Waverley novel is always constructed around a purely fictitious plot. Scott never stated the reasons for his practice, but one of them may have been a desire to avoid the historical stereotype likely to result from presenting the major historical figure performing the actions for which he is remembered. In general, historical personages play a larger part in Scott's later novels—thus Charles II is one of the major characters of *Woodstock*—and the fact seems related to the comparative weakness of most of those works.

The sense of history in the earlier works, the "Scotch Novels," is not derived from a parade of historical figures across the pages, or from a profusion of antiquarian detail (although there is sometimes too much of it). It comes instead from the close relationship of the characters to their social, political, and economic background, so that, as with Fergus Mac-Ivor or Rob Roy, the reader feels that these individuals could not have existed at any other moment of history. Still more importantly, the sense of history depends on the involvement of the character in the historic event (most commonly a violent crisis, such as a revolution, or civil war) so that his own destiny is shaped by history. Thus in *Old Mortality* one senses from the first that Morton, despite his wish to live quietly and to avoid taking a side, cannot possibly escape the history of his time; he must be drawn into the conflict of Cavaliers and Covenanters.

For such writing, of course, a profound knowledge of the past was necessary, a knowledge which Scott had acquired by endless reading of histories, memoirs, and pamphlets and by collecting ballads and folklore of all kinds. In theory, at least, Scott was quite aware of the dangers of overwhelming the reader with his accumulated knowledge of the past. The historical novelist, he explained in his introduction to *Ivanhoe*, should not concentrate on the obsolete but should emphasize "that extensive neutral ground . . . of manners and sentiments which are common to us and to our ancestors, having been handed down unaltered from them to us, or which, arising out of the principles of our common nature, must have existed alike in either state of society."

As might be expected, Scott was not greatly concerned about pedantic accuracy in minutiae, such as the exact date of a battle or the details of a costume. His aim was to "seek for parallels, compare events, and endeavour to make out the general trend . . . beneath the surface conflicts." [30] If he achieved this insight, an occasional anachronism or error hardly mattered. Scott's conception of history was a good deal deeper than was general in his time, and he realized that party conflicts and political intrigues did not constitute the most significant facts. The point is well expressed in Scott's comment on the memoirs of Horace Walpole; they showed, said Scott, "how little those who live in public business, and of course in constant agitation and intrigue, know about the real and deep course of opinions and events." Such men as Walpole, "immersed in little political detail, and the struggling skirmish of party, seem to have lost sight of the great progressive movements of human affairs." And Scott compared them to a miller so absorbed in his work that he fails to notice the gradual rising of the stream until it sweeps his mill away.[31]

These "great progressive movements" are constantly in motion, even in periods of outward peace. And Scott conceives of any period of the past as a moment of transition, of conflict between still older and newer manners, beliefs, and values; and much of the interest of his novels derives from the resulting tension. It seems a natural corollary of such a view that Scott should never have held a Carlylean "great man" theory of history. His approach is closer to that of Tolstoy. Scott presents the "great" often enough, but "never in the act of consciously, rationally, and decisively guiding events." [32]

The proper subject for Scott's historical imagination was Scottish history during the eighteenth century. When he ventures much beyond this period, his imagination and sympathies flag; and he falls back on historical stereotypes, antiquarian details, and obsolete diction. *Old Mortality* represents the limit of his imaginative reach, and comparison of the Covenanters and Cavaliers of that novel with the Roundheads and Cavaliers of *Woodstock*, only thirty years earlier, proves the point. The latter are caricatures or stock types—thus, Wildrake is simply what his name suggests. As Scott increasingly turned toward a more remote past, his difficulties increased. The dilemma which he faced was well described by a contemporary reviewer who pointed out that a novelist describing a remote period might be perfectly accurate in details of costume, furniture, and so forth. "But when he came to represent the details of individual character and feeling, and to delineate the daily conduct, and report the ordinary conversation of his persons, he would find himself either frozen in among naked and barren generalities, or engaged with modern Englishmen in the masquerade habits of antiquity." [33] The proper subject for the historical novelist seems to be "history that is not purely history because the spirit that moved in it was not entirely dead." [34] For Scott, such a subject meant the history of his own country during the century before his birth.

Scott's influence on the historical novel was decisive, but it should be added that his work may also have had a profound effect on the writing of formal history. Certainly the great narrative historians of the century—Macaulay, Carlyle, Prescott, Parkman—who aimed at making history as concrete, picturesque, and exciting as fiction, owed a great debt to the Waverley Novels both for their methods and for the audience which bought their work. More importantly, Scott's novels probably broadened the concept of history to include social and cultural as well as political and military matters. "When once the canvas of fiction had been enlarged [by Scott's lower-class character]," the historian G. M. Young has observed, "the canvas of history could be enlarged too. Increasingly the aim of historians became not merely to compile a record of names and dates but to recreate a culture." [35]

The basic theme of Scott's most characteristic work is itself historical: the conflict of the past and present (the "present" of each particular novel, that is). Scott himself implied as much when he explained in his introduction to *The Fortunes of Nigel* that "the most picturesque period of history is that when the ancient rough and wild manners of a barbarous age are just becoming innovated upon and contrasted by the illumination of increased or revived learning and the instructions of renewed or reformed religion." Scott explains his attraction to such subjects by the range of character and incident which they presented, but his interest was undoubtedly more serious and philosophical. Such a contrast appears in every one of the "Scotch Novels" and also in many of the later works. Among the critics of Scott, this theme has been most memorably and completely expressed by Coleridge:

Scott's great merit . . . lies in the nature of the subject . . . the contest between the loyalists and their opponents [Coleridge is apparently thinking of Whigs and Jacobites] can never become obsolete, for it is the contest between religious adherence to the past and the ancient, the desire and admiration of permanence, on the one hand; and the passion for increase of knowledge, for truth, as the offspring of reason—in short, the mighty instincts of *progression* and *free agency*, on the other. In all subjects of deep and lasting interest, you will detect a struggle between two opposites, two polar forces, both of which are alike necessary to our human well-being, and necessary each to the continued existence of the other.

This conflict creates "that equilibrium in which our moral Being subsists; while the disturbance of the same constitutes our sense of life." [36] The "dark hero" is always associated with an older, more reckless, violent and also glamorous mode of life, and he, like the life he represents, necessarily perishes. The conflict is rich and suggestive, and its significance should not be limited to political attitudes. It may even be suggested, as Fiedler does, that the contrasting heroes represent 'the principles of obedience and subversion, the controlled life of the super-ego and the impulsive life of the id." [37] John Buchan has credited Scott with reviving memory of the two strands of Scottish history—"the aristocratic and Cavalier; the Covenanting and democratic"—and with preventing a newly prosperous and expanding Scotland from forgetting its past. But, if this were the primary interest of the novels, they would have had little popularity outside Scotland. The broader theme, suggested by Coleridge and elaborated by modern critics, accounts more adequately both for the immediate success and for the enduring appeal of the Waverley Novels.

Here, most probably, is the explanation of Scott's long-continued interest in the Jacobite movement. *Rob Roy, Waverley,* and *Redgauntlet* carry the story of Jacobitism through the unsuccessful risings of 1715 and 1745 and on to the time in the 1760's when it was on the point of degenerating into a harmless drinking of toasts to the "King over the water." Jacobitism had attempted, coming surprisingly near success, to restore the past and to re-establish Scotland as a separate kingdom. Intellectually, Scott believed that events had worked out for the best. He valued the new security and prosperity of Scotland and saw that his own age was more comfortable, more rational, and more humane than the past. Emotionally, however, he was a Jacobite; he was attracted by the glamour of the Stuarts (a quality so strikingly absent in the first three Georges), and he regretted the lost independence of Scotland, a loss which seemed to endanger all of its national characteristics and institutions. (For similar reasons Scott disliked such reformers as Jeffrey, who seemed to him to be trying to destroy everything which made Scotland, Scotland.) The tension created in the works themselves is rooted in this division of sympathy—this split between head and heart—in the author.

Undoubtedly Scott's sense of history was inseparably related to his lifelong Toryism. His political thought seems to derive directly from Edmund Burke; like Burke, he is prepared to accept and defend the results of past revolutions, but he deplores all further change. Out of the conflicting fanaticisms of the past had emerged, in characteristically British fashion, a sensible middle way—one often represened by Scott's heroes and institutionalized by the Glorious Revolution of 1688 which, for him, had achieved a final settlement of the political and social order. His essential conservatism is aptly illustrated by his attitude toward the French Revolution. Unlike all of the other major romantic writers, Scott never indicated the least sympathy for the Revolution or its aims. "Bliss was it in that dawn to be alive" for Wordsworth and Coleridge; but, while they were still enthusiastic supporters of the Revolution, the young Scott was drilling with the Edinburgh Volunteers to repel any French invasion and to intimidate the lower classes.

Scott, never an "intellectual" in the usual sense of the word, was skeptical of the whiggish and liberal reliance on the power of reason and abstract thought to achieve political progress. In 1810 he published a highly Burkean "Essay on Judicial Reform" in which he warned against the danger of a purely rationalistic analysis of existing institutions or laws: "the people have, by degrees, moulded their habits to the law they are compelled to obey," and innovation raised great dangers of new and unforeseen evils.[38] The kind of insight which his philosophy of history allowed and the limitations which it imposed are both revealed by his remark in his journal entry for November 25, 1825 (apropos of the growing agitation for Catholic Emancipation and parliamentary reform); "The Whigs will live and die in the heresy that the world is ruled by little pamphlets and speeches," and that men only need to have their true interests explained to them in order to act accordingly. In reality, however, each man acts in accordance with his impulses regardless of his own or the general welfare. But, if nineteenth-century liberals were often disastrously in error as a result of failing to allow for the power of the irrational in politics (the history of the century provides abundant illustration of such error), Scott was seriously mistaken in denying the effect of ideas on history. Such a denial barred him from understanding the "great progressive movements" of his own time, and prevented him from recognizing in particular the significance of the French Revolution.

An essential part of Scott's Toryism was an intense respect for order and degree as necessary to a stable society. In this respect, at least, he is thoroughly Shakespearean, though his admirers have never pointed out the similarity. Scott had a profound respect for the Duke of Buccleuch, the traditional head of the Scott clan (although there was not the slightest legal obligation); and at Abbotsford Scott seems to have intended to create a feudal estate in which his people would owe him unquestioning loyalty and obedience, while he in turn would be morally obliged to guard their spiritual and physical welfare and to shield them from dangerous ideas. The gloom of Scott's last years was due not only to his bankruptcy but also to the course of public events—to his dismay at the "insatiate appetite of innovation" [39] which characterized the age. Passage of the Reform Bill seemed to him to threaten social chaos. When in 1832 the Whig Lord of the Admiralty placed a frigate at Scott's disposal for his voyage to the Mediterranean, he commented in his journal: "Things are still in the hands of gentlemen; but woe is me. They have so undermined the state of society that it will hardly keep together when they cease to be at the head of it."

Scott is equally conservative in his moral and religious thought

The moral code of the Waverley Novels is a strict and essentially puritan one based on restraint and self-denial. Anthony Trollope praised Scott for the strain he "put upon himself so that he should not be carried away into the seducing language of ill-regulated passion," [40] and certainly such language is absent from the novels. One does not feel, however, that excluding it imposed any "strain" on Scott. His heroes are never seriously tempted by "ill-regulated passion," and Scott's biographers provide no evidence that the author himself was ever so tempted. Scott's religious beliefs, it might be added, seem, in an eighteenth-century way, to have been superficial and conventional. A passage in *Waverley* is most revealing: "This worthy man . . . preached the practical fruits of Christianity as well as its abstract tenets." This sentence roused Coleridge to indignation: "*Abstract tenets*—i.e., whatever in the Gospel is peculiar to the Gospel! O what an opening into the actual state of religion among the higher classes. . . . Christ's Divinity, the Fall of Man, Sin, Redemption—abstract tenets!" [41] Scott would hardly have understood such objections. He had no interest in theology, and his religion was unemotional; he seems to have valued it chiefly as a necessary protection for morality and the social order. His own deepest belief, often expressed in his journal during his last years, was a stoical acceptance of whatever might come—an entirely non-Christian fatalism. Characteristically, he seems not to have noticed any inconsistency between this attitude and his formal religious professions; at any rate, he never attempted to reconcile these opposing positions.

Hazlitt's comment, in *The Spirit of the Age,* that "The old world is to him a crowded map; the new one a dull, hateful blank. He dotes on all well-authenticated superstitions; he shudders at the shadow of innovation" is melodramatic but essentially correct. And there probably is truth also in Hazlitt's opinion that this conservatism aided Scott's popularity: "The political bearing of the Scotch Novels has been a considerable recommendation to them. They are a relief to the mind, rarified as it has been with modern philosophy, and heated with ultra-radicalism." Hazlitt's suggestion is amusingly supported by Stendhal's novel *La Chartreuse de Parme,* whose hero is forbidden, during the intellectual reaction that followed the defeat of Napoleon, to read any book written later than 1715—except the Waverley Novels!

This conservatism profoundly influenced the novels in their moral standards and in their basic values. The Scott hero, it has been observed, is not so much Everyman as every gentleman; and, as a British gentleman of the early nineteenth century (whatever his ostensible period or country), he must display extreme respect for property, law, and the constituted authorities. A Waverley novel usually ends with the hero's acquiring a large amount of real estate by inheritance or by marriage. Mere money will not do; he must become a landed proprietor, and he cannot *earn* his wealth. Although Scott approved of commerce in the abstract, he seems not to have regarded even a successful businessman like his publisher Constable as quite a gentleman, and he realized the possible subversive effect of earned wealth on the social hierarchy.

In this conservatism lies an explanation of the curious passivity of the Scott hero, whose respect for the rights of property and the power of the established authority is so exaggerated that it paralyzes him. This is why Scott could never make one of his heroes into a convincing rebel, even when circumstances seemed to require it. Waverley and Henry Morton do join rebellions, to be sure, but only through overwhelming force of circumstances; and they are thoroughly uncomfortable until other circumstances have disengaged them.

"Life could not be endured were it seen in reality," Scott wrote in his journal in 1825; and he speculated, "What a strange scene if the surge of conversation could suddenly ebb like the tide and show us the state of people's real minds." Ordinarily, however, Scott made no attempt to penetrate very far below the social mask. Critics have frequently complained of a lack of depth in Scott's characters, and some of his extreme admirers have even, rather ridiculously, made a virtue out of this deficiency. "He was too manly even to publish his feelings," writes one; and he adds that Scott had a "fine reticence that forbade his disclosing either his own innermost personal feelings or those of his characters." [42] Grierson's suggestion seems at least plausible since certainty in such matters is unattainable: "If he did not enter very deeply into the souls of the characters whom he drew, it was because he never entered very deeply into his own motives. . . . It is this dislike of analyzing feeling that makes his heroes of so little interest." [43]

Scott was the least introspective of writers. He was so ignorant of his own nature that, after ten years of extravagant spending, soon to end in a spectacular bankruptcy, he could solemnly advise his eldest son: "you must learn to keep all your expenses within your income; it is a lesson which, if not learned in youth, lays up much bitter regret for age." [44] The novels are surprisingly lacking in autobiographical detail; Scott never wrote a *David Copperfield* or a *Pendennis*. This lack of intimacy, both in regard to himself and his characters, may have been caused, as Edwin Muir has suggested, by an early and unsuccessful love affair. In any case, the fact exists; and such extreme reticence cannot be considered a virtue in a novelist, whatever it may be in a gentleman.

Scott's lack of interest in himself is paralleled by his unconcern, except when he had been commissioned to write a review, with esthetic issues. For this reason, his letters make dull reading; they reveal nothing either of his inner life or of his literary problems. Croce has complained that Scott's biographers seem to be dealing with a captain of industry rather than a writer. They "illustrate and admire his sagacity of invention, his diligence, which enabled him to write two or three stories every year, the castle which he was able to build . . . nothing is said as to his inner life, his loves, his religion, his ideas; less than nothing as to his spiritual struggles and development." [45] But, apparently, the fault is not with the biographers but with their subject and the materials available to them. Thus Grierson's biography, the most factually reliable, is principally a record of contracts, sales of books, and purchases of property. Scott himself, as we have seen, regarded his novels as a kind of industrial product, and judged them solely by their commercial success. "It is a singular fact," says Lockhart, "that before the public, or rather the booksellers, had given their decision, he no more knew whether he had written well or ill, than whether a die thrown out of a box was to turn up a size or an ace." [46] There could be no more damaging admission about a creative writer.

Evidence of Scott's thoroughgoing commercialism is abundant. According to Grierson, *The Lady of the Lake* was the last major work which Scott wrote for his own satisfaction as well as for profit: "Thereafter almost everything he wrote was with a view to meet engagements already incurred, to cancel or renew bills falling due . . ." [47] Carlyle's comment on the Waverley Novels, that

"The great fact about them is that they were faster written and better paid for than any other books in the world," [48] merely states what to Scott was the evidence of his success. The last word on the artistic deficiencies of the Waverley Novels and their cause may be left to Scott himself. He is writing of Dryden, but if one substitutes "novels" for "dramas" the following passage applies perfectly to his own work: "Laboured accuracy of expression, and fine traits of character, joined to an action which should be at once pleasing, interesting, and probable, required sedulous study, deep reflection, and long and repeated correction and revision. But these were not to be expected from a playwright, by whom three dramas were to be produced in one season; and in their place were substituted adventures, surprises, rencounters, mistakes, disguises, and escapes." [49]

To many readers, esthetic and moral issues are not only irrelevant to the enjoyment of fiction but troublesome—adventures, surprises, mistakes, and escapes are precisely what they require. Such readers are disturbed by concern with form, by melancholy or passion, by seriousness of any kind. To them, art would only spoil the fun. Coleridge assumed that the weaknesses of the Waverley Novels were essential to their popularity, and pointed out that Scott's fiction made fewer demands on the reader than the great eighteenth-century novels: "The absence of the higher beauties and excellencies of style, character, and plot has done more for Sir Walter Scott's European . . . popularity, than ever the abundance of them effected for any former writer." [50] In an "age of anxiety" (Coleridge's own phrase) like the early nineteenth century, readers sought escape, on the easiest terms, through fiction; and Scott supplied it. The Waverley Novels of course contained ingredients lacking in contemporary Gothic fiction, in the novel of manners, and also in the eighteenth-century classics, most obviously in the novelty of their settings and of the "manners" described. Scott did not originate, but successfully exploited, the intellectual reaction against both rationalism and Jacobinism as well as the increased regard for tradition and the past—the growing sense of nationalism and interest in the history of one's own nation or region.

Subsidiary reasons for his success are easy to suggest. No doubt the mystery of at least theoretically anonymous authorship added to public curiosity and kept the novels under discussion. As Carlyle, a contemporary, described it, "The Waverley Novels circulated and reigned triumphant; to the general imagination the 'Author of Waverley' was like some living mythological personage and ranked among the chief wonders of the world." [51] In his respect for propriety Scott was much superior to his eighteenth-century predecessors—a matter of great importance in an age of tightening moral standards, when Victorianism was only a few years distant and when reading aloud to family or friends was a favorite amusement. Scott was not only proper, he was a gentleman, and that, as Adolphus pointed out, was a distressingly rare quality among contemporary authors: "How few are there who give any proof in their works of the refined taste, the instinctive sense of propriety, the clear spirit of honour . . . the familiar acquaintance with conventional forms of good breeding, which are essential to the character of a gentleman!" [52]

But the most important cause of success, no doubt, was that the novels offered such perfect escape. A character like Rob Roy, Fiedler points out, "projects the bourgeois' own slight margin of resentment against the safe, commercial way of life he has desired, and for which, indeed, he would fight. . . . Such tame outsiders represent the impulsive and the irrational only as a passing temptation . . . not as a profound threat." [53] A Waverley or a Frank Osbaldistone may tour the wild Highlands and feel the dangerous glamour of a dark hero, but he soon returns (with souvenirs and sentimental regrets, to be sure) to England or to the Lowlands, and to common sense and respectability.

It is likely, however, that the causes of such phenomenal literary success can never be completely explained. Scott's contemporaries were sometimes puzzled by the popularity of the Waverley Novels. The comment in the *Quarterly Review* on *The Lord of the Isles* applies equally to the novels. Scott, says the reviewer, "infuses into his narrative such a flow of life, and . . . animal spirits, that without satisfying the judgment, or moving the feelings, or elevating the mind, or even greatly exciting the curiosity, he is able to seize upon the imagination of his readers in a manner which is often truly unaccountable." [54] With this statement we must leave this problem.

III *Criticism*

Criticism of the Waverley Novels began at once, with publication of *Waverley* in 1814, and it continued in an abundant stream through the nineteenth century, then in steadily diminishing volume into the twentieth. His contemporaries, with only a few exceptions like Coleridge, had no doubt that he was the greatest of novelists. To express their sense of his greatness, they paid him the highest honor they could imagine—they compared him with Shakespeare, a comparison which became standard for many years, and is still made by such admirers as Grierson and Daiches. Scott wrote historical novels and Shakespeare had written historical plays; both were prolific and rapid writers, assumed to be careless about revision (Shakespeare, we remember, is supposed to have "never blotted a line"); both are assumed to have taken a strictly commercial view of their art (that Scott did we know, but there is not the slightest evidence concerning Shakespeare's attitude toward his plays). Often the comparison turns out to be a critical strategy for reducing the significance of Scott's weaknesses, or even turning them into virtues, by attributing them to Shakespeare.

In any case, the differences of period and of medium—not to mention accomplishment—make the comparison unilluminating. When it is pushed beyond the broadest generalities, it simply will not stand examination. Grierson remarks that *Old Mortality* is "the kind of story which was his, and Shakespeare's, normal method of presenting life and history—a broadly delineated chapter of history with strongly marked characters, natural and intelligible, but not too deeply or subtly analyzed." [55] The statement is true of the author of *Waverley*, but is it true of the author of *Hamlet?* Undoubtedly, as has been mentioned previously, Scott owed a debt to Shakespeare's histories for the general plan of his own novels and for some of his characters as well; but this indebtedness is a different matter.

Comparisons with Cervantes have been made by Grierson and others, and perhaps there is more justification for so doing. Scott's knowledge of human nature, Grierson declares, at the risk of contradicting himself, was, "if not subtle and profound, yet wide and just and sympathetic, more akin in its range and limitations to the genius of Cervantes than of Shakespeare." [56] Scott was familiar with *Don Quixote*, and there is a similarity of theme in much of his work: "Novel after novel presents an illusioned, romantic young man pursuing a series of exotic adventures in a dreamlike trance . . . Eventually . . . he comes out of his dream with a sensation of sadness and loss." [57] Waverley is no doubt the purest example of such an "illusioned" young man. We might mention also the shrewd, practical, selfish servants who sometimes accompany their idealistic and "romantic" young masters as Sancho Panza accompanies the Don. None of Scott's novels presents this theme with anything like the consistency and clarity with which Cervantes presented it, yet the similarity is suggestive, and might reward scholarly investigation.

Homer too has been used for comparison (at least one critic has compared Scott simultaneously with Shakespeare, Cervantes, and Homer), on the assumption that Homer, like Scott and also like Shakespeare and Cervantes, is an example of the spontaneously creative "maker" who contrasts with the meticulous, self-conscious artist. Such comparisons, however, are too remote to have any real critical value; and they are likely to diminish Scott to modern readers by reminding them of how great the disparity in accomplishment is.

Coleridge seems the most penetrating and original of Scott's contemporary critics, but his comments were private and disconnected and could not influence the general attitude. Well before Scott's death, a critical consensus about his work had been reached: "His characters are superior to his plots; his humble, to his higher life; his Scotland to his England; his tragedy to his comedy; and, in general, his earlier to his later works." [58] Deficiencies in plotting and slovenliness of style were admitted, but considered of little importance. In general, this attitude prevailed throughout the century, reinforced by the wide admiration for Scott's character which developed during his life; and this view was strongly reinforced by Lockhart's biography. Carlyle's vicious attack, published as a review of Lockhart, was the most striking exception. Carlyle charged Scott with commercialism, with superficiality of characterization, with writing by formula (he "manufacturers" rather than "creates"), and above all with the absence of a message or an idea for his readers: he 'wished not the world to elevate itself, to amend itself, to do this or to do that, except simply pay him for books he kept writing." [59]

Scott's artistic failings were first emphasized by Edward Bulwer-Lytton (an unlikely source!), later and more tellingly by Robert Louis Stevenson, who certainly owed a great debt to the Waverley Novels. Scott, for Stevenson, was a "great daydreamer" rather than a great artist, or an artist at all: "he conjured up the romantic with delight but had hardly the patience to describe it." [60] His style was incompetent, and his episodes were not satisfactorily dramatized. One might wonder what was left, after such a wholesale dismissal; but Stevenson did not face that question.

Twentieth-century criticism of Scott, on the whole, has declined in quantity and in interest. The major English and American critics, with a few exceptions, have apparently not found Scott's novels interesting enough to write about. One of the exceptions is E. M. Forster, who in his *Aspects of the Novel* has made the most sustained attack on the Waverley Novels. Scott, he believes, has "a trivial mind, and a heavy style. He cannot construct. He has neither artistic detachment nor passion, and how can a writer who is devoid of both, create characters who will move us deeply? . . . think how all Scott's laborious mountains and scooped-out glens call out for passion, passion and how it is never there! . . . he only has temperate and gentlemanly feelings and an intelligent affection for the country-side; and this is not basis enough for great novels." [61] Evidence enough has been given to establish Scott's lack of "artistic detachment." The absence of "passion" may be traced to the moral code which Scott accepted and which governs his novels, and to the repressions and inhibitions of his own personality, as Muir has suggested. In any case, the absence is a fact that is obvious if we compare any Waverley novel with *Wuthering Heights*. Forster's conclusion, that "to make one thing happen after another is his only serious aim," seems essentially true; and it might very well have been admitted by Scott himself. Even more damaging, perhaps, is the tolerant dismissal of a critic like Benedetto Croce, in his *European Literature in the Nineteenth Century*, whose views may be taken as representative of European criticism in the twentieth century, in so far as it has concerned itself with Scott at all. Let us be respectful toward Scott, says Croce in effect, for he delighted our ancestors. Artistic criteria, however, are irrelevant to a discussion of his novels. The view of F. R. Leavis is similar although it is expressed in surprisingly mild terms from a critic noted for severity. Leavis considers Scott "a kind of inspired folklorist"—not very different from Forster's phrase, "an intelligent affection for the country-side"; and he finds that "the heroics of the historical novel can no longer command respect. He was a great and very intelligent man; but, not having the creative writer's interest in literature, he made no serious attempt to work out his own form . . . *The Heart of Midlothian* comes the nearest to being a great novel, but hardly *is* that: too many allowances and deductions have to be made." [62] The only parts of Scott's work which retain any vitality for Leavis are "The Two Drovers" and "Wandering Willie's Tale."

It is easily noticeable that much of the favorable recent comment on Scott seems to be motivated by an indiscriminate rejection of modern art. Even as reputable a critic as Grierson provides a gross example of this kind of philistinism: "One might divide writers of today into those who refuse and denounce, and those who accept and enjoy human nature and human life: Ibsen, Hardy, and many of the Russian and French novelists and their followers; while on the other side are the inheritors of the genial, kindly humanity of a Chaucer, a Cervantes, a Scott. Which is better, each reader must decide for himself." [63] Grierson has obviously decided, as his loaded statement indicates. Such criticism distorts the work of the writers whom it condemns and trivializes that of the writers it admires. Another admirer, S. C. Roberts, in the same series of Scott Lectures, points out, "the great gulf between Scott and those modern novelists who spend so much time prying into their characters that they frequently forget that they may be expected to tell a story." [64] Such critical stupidity is likely only to damage the reputation of Scott.

It is not surprising that not only most of the recent favorable criticism of Scott, but most of the criticism of any kind, comes from his countrymen, who have a natural interest in Scott's subject matter and a patriotic enthusiasm for his reputation as one of the two great writers of modern Scotland—as the prose counterpart of Robert Burns. Scott himself provided an explanation of this kind of popularity in commenting on the appeal of "our popular poetry: Much of its peculiar charm is . . . to be attributed solely to its *locality.*" And readers "are charmed by the effect of local description, and sometimes impute that effect to the poet, which is produced by the recollections and associations which his verses excite." [65]

It is certainly a striking paradox that some of the lengthiest and most sympathetic criticism of the intensely conservative Scott should have been written by Georg Lukacs, the Hungarian Communist and probably the best-known Marxist critic of our time. Lukacs' interest derives from Scott's sympathetic presentation of characters drawn from the lower classes and, of course, from Scott's use of historical subjects and particularly his tendency to treat a historical crisis as a kind of dialectical conflict between opposite forces resulting finally in a new synthesis. Thus in *Ivanhoe* the conflict of Saxon and Norman produces the Englishman, represented by Wilfrid of Ivanhoe. In his *The Historical Novel,* Lukacs discusses the historical implications of the Waverley Novels more thoroughly than any other critic has done, but has nothing of interest to say about their esthetic qualities.

It does not seem likely that the Waverley Novels will ever again be widely read, although they may continue, very understandably, to be the objects of patriotic enthusiasm in Scotland. The steady decline of interest in Scott's work in the twentieth century seems not to result merely from "literary fads" or from the prejudice of a few influential critics, like the temporary depreciation of Milton as a result of the hostility of Leavis and Eliot, but to proceed from the recognition of radical flaws in his work—flaws which make it improbable that Scott will triumphantly re-emerge from obscurity in the manner of Herman Melville or John Donne. Serious critics of the novel will feel that, in Leavis' words, "too many allowances and deductions have to be made." On the other hand, the reader who asks nothing more than temporary escape from his own life has available in books and other media innumerable sources of amusement and self-forgetfulness requiring far less time and effort than the Waverley Novels.

It will not do to say, as Walter Allen does in his recent history of the English novel, that "Scott was a great writer of fiction who was never a good novelist." [66] The paradox is unacceptable, since fiction cannot exist apart from the works which contain it. Yet no student of literature and of the novel (not merely the English novel) can afford to ignore the work of Scott. In summarizing Scott's influence, Allen had credited it with three principal effects: "He made the European novel"; "he revolutionized the writing of history"; and, "in religion . . . he lay behind the Oxford movement." To an American reader, the order may seem anticlimactic, but Scott's work undoubtedly exerted a significant effect on the minds of men like Newman and Ruskin and encouraged the fashionable medievalism of the Victorian Age.

IV *Influence on the Novel*

Since Scott's influence on the writing of history has already been briefly considered, we should turn our attention to Allen's first claim—"He made the European novel." To a surprising extent, the statement is literally true. The first important modern Italian novel, Manzoni's *The Betrothed,* is a historical novel obviously inspired by the Waverley Novels. In Russia, Scott's influence led directly to the first significant Russian novel, Alexander Pushkin's *The Captain's Daughter*, which deals with a popular uprising in the eighteenth century, just the sort of subject typical of Scott. One might think also of Nikolai Gogol's novel of seventeenth-century Cossack life, *Taras Bulba,* as well as of Tolstoy's *War and Peace.* In Poland, somewhat later, there are the novels of Henryk Sienkiewicz that present Poland's successful struggle for survival during the seventeenth century against apparently hopeless odds, reminding the Poles of their national identity and their heroic past. The political and cultural influence of the Waverley Novels on the suppressed nationalities of Eastern Europe must have been considerable.

In France, Scott's popularity was enormous. The uncritical enthusiasm of the public was satirized by a contemporary: "By Walter Scott! By Walter Scott! Hurry, gentlemen, and especially ladies; it's marvelous, it's new; hurry! The first edition is exhausted, the second is sold in advance, the third will disappear as soon as it leaves the press. Run, buy; good or bad, what does it matter! Sir Walter Scott has put his name to it, and that's enough." [67] It was not to be expected that the effect of the Waverley Novels should be as decisive on French literature as on a literature still in its formative state, like that of Russia; but, even so, Scott's influence is clear in the historical fiction not only of Alexander Dumas but of Victor Hugo, Alfred de Vigny, Prosper Merimée and Théophile Gautier among others. Even a novelist as temperamentally opposite to Scott as Stendhal seems to have been affected. Stendhal's *La Chartreuse de Parme* is certainly a kind of historical novel and the famous description of the hero, Fabrizio, at Waterloo (Fabrizio never glimpses his idol, Napoleon, and never fires a shot at the enemy) may well have been suggested by Scott's frequently oblique approach to a great historic event or figure.

Scott's influence was not limited to Europe. The American novel really begins with Cooper—the "American Scott"—and Cooper owes everything—style, subject, character types—to Scott. At one remove, Scott's influence was also decisive on William Gilmore Simms, the "Southern Cooper." Less obvious, yet real, is the debt of Nathaniel Hawthorne, who throughout his life delighted in the Waverley Novels. Hawthorne's early and abortive project, "Seven Tales of My Native Land," was an attempt to do for New England's past what Scott had done for Scotland's; and in *The Scarlet Letter,* as well as many of his finest tales, Hawthorne accomplished his purpose. One might mention the similarities between Hawthorne's Puritans and Scott's Covenanters, and the parallelism of Hawthorne's town-forest contrast, especially as developed in *The Scarlet Letter* and in "Young Goodman Brown," with Scott's favorite Lowland-Highland juxtaposition. Scott reminded writers of all Western nations of the unique value of their own national pasts, and major novels in many languages (along, inevitably, with numerous plagiarisms) resulted.

Naturally, Scott's influence on the English novel was profound. Some critics, even though favorably disposed, have seen that influence as harmful. Walter Allen blames Scott for foisting on the nineteenth-century English novel the "arbitrary, complicated plot" and "unreal, romantic heroes and heroines"; and he sums up Scott's harmful effects: "His defects of form and artistic laziness became . . . authoritative in the novel for two generations after him." [68] Scott, however, hardly originated the complicated plot or the unreal hero, although it is arguable that his example increased their currency. The complex plot, in any case, was put to excellent use by some Victorian novelists.

Scott's influence on English fiction is more direct and positive, and it does not lie mainly in the work of his imitators, the most important of whom is Stevenson. It does not lie even in his example as historical novelist, although the historical novel was attempted, without great success, by Dickens, Thackeray, George Eliot, Hardy—all of the major Victorian novelists, in short. First, Scott made regional peculiarities of custom and dialect acceptable in serious fiction, whereas in the eighteenth-century novel, as in earlier drama, such characteristics had invariably been considered as inherently clownish and comic. If we associate, for example, Hardy with Wessex or George Eliot and D. H. Lawrence with the Midlands, it is because Scott had provided the example with his treatment of Lowland types who speak their native dialect.

Closely related is a second, and perhaps even more important point—Scott's serious treatment of characters from the lower classes. One could say without much exaggeration that in earlier literature it was apparently impossible to treat such characters seriously. They had been generally either clowns, like the commoners in Shakespeare, or the idealized nymphs and swains of pastoral. We must therefore, imagine the startling novelty of a Bailie Jarvie, a David Deans, or a Dandie Dinmont. Contemporary readers, quite aware of the novelty, responded according to their temperaments. The more conservative, like a *Blackwood's* reviewer of *The Heart of Midlothian,* found far too much about "the concerns of a cowfeeder and his daughter" and regretted such a tendency to deal "not only with low, but with vulgar life" whereby the Muse had "soiled her petticoats, if not dimmed her beauty." [69] Another reviewer, writing in the more liberal *Edinburgh Review,* noted the paradox that, in spite of his "propensities decidedly aristocratic," Scott succeeded best "in the representation of homely characters;—and not in the ludicrous or contemptuous representation of them—but by showing them at once more natural and more interesting than they had ever been made before . . . by showing them not as clowns to be laughed at . . . but as human creatures." "The finer attributes that are ascribed to them," the reviewer notes, "are so blended and harmonized with the native rudeness of their life and occupations, that they are made interesting and even noble beings . . . and delight us without trespassing at all on the province of pastoral or romance." [70] Scott achieved in fiction what Wordsworth had attempted, with mixed success, in the poems of *Lyrical Ballads*. Something may be owing to his Scottish background—Burns's poetry was far more democratic and socially inclusive than any English poetry of the eighteenth century, or even Wordsworth's.

In these respects, then, Scott was a great innovator: he developed the historical novel, and he made possible serious presentation of regional characteristics and of characters from social levels below the aristocracy and the upper-middle class. He significantly widened the range of fiction, even though he may have failed to find the proper form for his innovations, with the result that his own work is no longer part of the living novel. But, if Scott has become purely a historical figure, he is unquestionably a major one.

Notes and References

Chapter Two

1. H. J. C. Grierson, *Sir Walter Scott*, Bart. (London, 1938), p. 76.
2. John Gibson Lockhart, *Memoirs of the Life of Sir Walter Scott* (New York, 1901), I, p. 419.
3. Cited in *Scott's Complete Poetical Works*, ed. H. E. Scudder (New York, 1900), p. 39.
4. Grierson, p. 81.
5. Lockhart, II, p. 32.
6. *The Letters of Wm. and Dorothy Wordsworth: The Middle Years*, ed. E. DeSelincourt (Oxford, 1937), I, p. 240.
7. Lockhart, II, p. 171.
8. *Complete Poetical Works*, p. 152.
9. *Ibid.*, p. 153.
10. *Collected Letters of Samuel Taylor Coleridge*, ed. E. L. Griggs (Oxford, 1959), III, p. 291.
11. John L. Adolphus, *Letters to Richard Heber, Esq.* (London, 1822), p. 132.
12. *Coleridge the Talker*, ed. R. W. Armour and R. F. Howes (Ithaca: Cornell University Press, 1940), p. 171.
13. H. J. C. Grierson and J. C. Smith, *A Critical History of English Poetry* (New York, 1946), p. 367.
14. John Speirs, *The Scots Literary Tradition* (London, 1952), p. 120.

Chapter Three

1. Sir Walter Scott, *Lives of the Novelists* (London, 1906), p. 21. (Subsequent references to this edition will appear in the text.)
2. John Gibson Lockhart, *Memoirs of the Life of Sir Walter Scott* (New York, 1901), III, p. 16.
3. *The Journal of Sir Walter Scott* (New York, 1890), I, p. 85.
4. Lockhart, IV, p. 456.
5. *Journal*, I, p. 117.
6. Lockhart, III, p. 22.
7. *Journal*, I, p. 54.

8. Quoted in Hesketh Pearson, *Sir Walter Scott: His Life and Personality* (New York, 1954), p. 242.

9. *Journal*, II, p. 276.

10. Review of *Emma, The Quarterly Review*, XIV, (1815), p. 199.

11. *Ibid.*, p. 195.

12. *Ibid.*, p. 197.

13. Review of *Frankenstein, Blackwood's Magazine*, II (1818), p. 613.

14. Ian Watt, *The Rise of the Novel: Studies in Defoe, Richardson and Fielding* (Berkeley, 1959), p. 32.

15. Review of *Frankenstein*, p. 614.

16. Lockhart, IV, p. 153.

17. Margaret Ball, *Sir Walter Scott as a Critic of Literature* (New York, 1907), p. 109.

18. "Historical Romance," *The Quarterly Review*, XXXV (1827), p. 529.

19. Meyer Abrams, *The Mirror and the Lamp: Romantic Theory and the Critical Tradition* (New York, 1953), p. 15.

20. Review of *Emma, The Quarterly Review*, XIV (1815), p. 193.

21. Review of *The Omen* (by John Galt), *Blackwood's Magazine*. XX (1826), p. 57.

22. Lockhart, IV, p. 176.

23. *Journal*, II, p. 111.

24. *Ibid.*, I, p. 155.

Chapter Four

1. Sir Walter Scott, "General Preface to the Waverley Novels."

2. *Ibid.*

3. *Ibid.*

4. Review of *Waverley, The Quarterly Review* (July, 1814), p. 377.

5. Review of *Waverley, Edinburgh Review* (November, 1814), p. 208.

6. Lockhart, II, pp. 534–35.

7. *Jane Austen's Letters to Her Sister Cassandra and Others*, ed. R. W. Chapman (London, 1952), p. 404.

8. Lockhart, II, p. 396.

9. James T. Hillhouse, *The Waverley Novels and Their Critics* (Minneapolis, 1936), p. 112.

10. *Sir Walter Scott Lectures*, ed. H. J. C. Grierson (Edinburgh, 1950), pp. 125–26.

11. Adolphus, p. 160.

12. *The Letters of Sir Walter Scott*, ed. H. J. C. Grierson (London, 1932), I, p. 342.

13. Review of *Waverley, The Quarterly Review*, p. 377.

14. D. D. Devlin, "Scott and Redgauntlet," *Review of English Literature* (January, 1963), p. 91.

15. John Buchan, *Sir Walter Scott* (London, 1932), p. 264.

16. David Daiches, "Scott's *Redgauntlet*," in *From Jane Austen to Joseph Conrad*, ed. R. C. Rathbun and Martin Steinmann (Minneapolis, 1958), p. 54.

17. Daiches, "Scott's *Redgauntlet*," p. 56.

Chapter Five

1. Lockhart, III, pp. 25–26.

2. Andrew Lang, Preface to *Guy Mannering* in the Border Edition of the Waverley Novels (London, 1898).

3. Welsh, p. 212.

4. Lockhart, III, p. 104.

5. *Ibid.*, III, pp. 103–4.

6. Henry James, "The Art of Fiction."

7. Lockhart, III, p. 105.

Chapter Six

1. Lockhart, III, p. 134.

2. *Ibid.*, III, p. 131.

3. Scott, *Letters*, IV, p. 293.

4. Adolphus, p. 200.

5. Lockhart, III, p. 121.

6. Georg Lukacs, *The Historical Novel* (London, 1962), p. 35.

7. Review of *Tales of My Landlord* in *The Edinburgh Review* (March, 1817), p. 216.

8. Georg Lukacs, *The Historical Novel* (London, 1962), pp. 36–37.

9. David Daiches, *Literary Essays* (Edinburgh & London, 1956), p. 110.

10. Lockhart, III, p. 134.

Chapter Seven

1. Buchan, p. 181.

2. *Ibid.*, p. 183.

3. S. T. Coleridge, *Miscellaneous Criticism*, ed. T. M. Raysor (Cambridge: Harvard University Press, 1936), p. 323.

4. Buchan, p. 184.

5. Leslie Fiedler, *Love and Death in the American Novel* (New York, 1960), p. 167.

6. David Craig, *Scottish Literature and the Scottish People, 1680–1830* (London, 1961), p. 147.

7. Lockhart, III, p. 130.
8. *Ibid.*, III, p. 126.
9. Buchan, p. 192.

Chapter Eight

1. Lockhart, III, p. 267.
2. Buchan, p. 188.
3. Cited in Grierson, p. 165.
4. Robin Mayhead, "*The Heart of Midlothian:* Scott as Artist," *Essays in Criticism* (July, 1956), p. 266.
5. Mayhead, p. 268.
6. P. F. Fisher, "Providence, Fate and the Historical Imagination in Scott's *The Heart of Midlothian,*" in *Nineteenth Century Fiction* (September, 1955), p. 114.
7. Craig, p. 217.
8. Dorothy Van Ghent, *The English Novel: Form and Function* (New York, 1953), p. 120.
9. Joan H. Pittock, "*The Heart of Midlothian:* Scott as Artist?", *Essays in Criticism* (April, 1957), p. 479.

Chapter Nine

1. Grierson, p. 182.
2. Coleridge, p. 334.
3. Lockhart, IV, p. 151.
4. *Ibid.*
5. Buchan, p. 302.
6. Coleridge, p. 300.
7. Adolphus, p. 200.
8. Welsh, p. 223.
9. Adolphus, p. 201.
10. *Ibid.*
11. Welsh, p. 58.
12. Review of *The Fortunes of Nigel, The Quarterly Review* (July, 1822), p. 339.
13. Review of *Tales of My Landlord, The Quarterly Review* (January, 1817), p. 432.
14. Lukacs, pp. 36–37.
15. Daiches, p. 86.
16. *Ibid.*, 93–94.
17. Lockhart, III, p. 417.
18. Craig, p. 151.
19. Coleridge, p. 136.

20. E. M. W. Tillyard, *The Epic Strain in the English Novel* (London, 1958), p. 78.

21. Virginia Woolf, *The Moment* (New York, 1948), p. 63.

22. Cited in Craig, 250.

23. Review of *Tales of My Landlord* in *The Edinburgh Review* (March, 1817), p. 198.

24. Craig, p. 56.

25. *Ibid.*, p. 57.

26. Review of *Tales of My Landlord* in *The Edinburgh Review* (March, 1817), p. 198.

27. Carlyle, p. 26.

28. Daiches, p. 156.

29. Review of *Tales of My Landlord, The Quarterly Review*, p. 431.

30. Review of *The Fortunes of Nigel, The Edinburgh Review* (June, 1825), p. 223.

31. Duncan Forbes, "The Rationalism of Sir Walter Scott," *The Cambridge Journal* (October, 1953), p. 26.

32. Lockhart, IV, p. 8.

33. Forbes, p. 32.

34. Review of *Ivanhoe, The Edinburgh Review* (January, 1820), p. 7.

35. Grierson, p. 181.

36. *Sir Walter Scott Lectures,* ed. H. J. C. Grierson (Edinburgh, 1950), p. 103.

37. Coleridge, *Miscellaneous Criticism*, pp. 341–42.

38. Fiedler, p. 167.

39. Cited in Lockhart, II, p. 210.

40. Lockhart, IV, p. 11.

41. Cited in Richard Stang, *The Theory of the Novel in England: 1850–1870* (New York, 1959), p. 202.

42. Coleridge, *Miscellaneous Criticism*, p. 322.

43. Thorlief Larsen, "The Classical Elements in Scott's Poetry," Transactions of the Royal Society of Canada, 3rd Series, sec. II, p. 115.

44. Grierson, p. 68.

45. Lockhart, IV, p. 72.

46. Benedetto Croce, *European Literature in the Nineteenth Century* (New York, 1924), p. 68.

47. Lockhart, III, p. 22.

48. Grierson, p. 89.

49. Carlyle, p. 83.

50. Sir Walter Scott, *The Works of John Dryden,* revised and corrected by George Saintsbury (Edinburgh, 1882), I, p. 63.

51. Coleridge, *Miscellaneous Criticism*, p. 335.

52. Carlyle, p. 26.

53. Adolphus, p. 41.

54. Fiedler, p. 154.

55. Cited in Lockhart, III, p. 20.

56. Grierson, p. 177.

57. Clell T. Peterson, *Romance and Realism in the Waverley Novels,* (unpublished doctoral dissertation at the University of Minnesota, 1962), p. 25.

58. Review of *Fortunes of Nigel, The Quarterly Review,* p. 337.

59. Carlyle, p. 54.

60. Robert Louis Stevenson, "A Gossip on Romance," in *Memories and Portraits* (London, 1904), p. 264.

61. E. M. Forster, *Aspects of the Novel* (New York, 1927), p. 52.

62. F. R. Leavis, *The Great Tradition* (London, 1948), p. 6.

63. *Scott Lectures,* p. 51.

64. *Ibid.,* p. 153.

65. *The Letters of Sir Walter Scott,* ed. H. J. C. Grierson (London, 1932), I, p. 146.

66. Walter Allen, *The English Novel: A Short Critical History* (New York, 1954).

67. Cited in Louis Maigron, *Le Roman Historique a L'Epoque Romantique* (Paris, 1912), p. 52.

68. Allen, p. 135.

69. Cited in Hillhouse, p. 57.

70. Review of *Tales of My Landlord* in *The Edinburgh Review* (March, 1817), p. 196.

Selected Bibliography

PRIMARY SOURCES

The Complete Poetical Works of Sir Walter Scott, ed. Horace E. Scudder. Boston: Houghton, Mifflin and Company, 1898. A convenient and thoroughly annotated edition.

The Journal of Sir Walter Scott, ed. J. G. Tait. Edinburgh: Oliver & Boyd, 1950.

The Letters of Sir Walter Scott, ed. H. J. C. Grierson. 12 vols. London: Constable and Company, 1932.

Lives of the Novelists. Oxford University Press, 1906.

Miscellaneous Works of Sir Walter Scott. 28 vols. Edinburgh: R. Cadell, 1834–36.

Waverley, or 'Tis Sixty Years Since. Edinburgh: A. Constable and Company, 1814.

Guy Mannering, or The Astrologer. Edinburgh: A. Constable and Company, 1815.

The Antiquary. Edinburgh: A. Constable and Company, 1816.

Tales of My Landlord [*The Black Dwarf* and *Old Mortality*]. Edinburgh: William Blackwood, 1816.

Tales of My Landlord. Second Series [*The Heart of Midlothian*] Edinburgh: A. Constable and Company, 1818.

Rob Roy. Edinburgh: A. Constable and Company, 1818.

Tales of My Landlord. Third Series [*The Bride of Lammermoor* and *A Legend of Montrose*]. Edinburgh: A. Constable and Company, 1819.

Ivanhoe. Edinburgh: A. Constable and Company, 1820.

The Monastery. Edinburgh: A. Constable and Company, 1820.

The Abbot. Edinburgh: A. Constable and Company, 1820.

Kenilworth. Edinburgh: A. Constable and Company, 1821.

The Pirate. Edinburgh: A. Constable and Company, 1822.

The Fortunes of Nigel. Edinburgh: A. Constable and Company, 1822.

Peveril of the Peak. Edinburgh: A. Constable and Company, 1822.

Quentin Durward. Edinburgh: A. Constable and Company, 1823.

St. Ronan's Well. Edinburgh: A. Constable and Company, 1823.

Selected Bibliography

Redgauntlet: A Tale of the Eighteenth Century. Edinburgh: A. Constable and Company, 1824.

Tales of the Crusaders [*The Betrothed* and *The Talisman*]. Edinburgh: A. Constable and Company, 1825.

Woodstock, or The Cavalier. Edinburgh: A. Constable and Company, 1826.

Chronicles of the Canongate, The Highland Widow, The Two Drovers, and The Surgeon's Daughter. Edinburgh: Cadell and Company, 1827.

Chronicles of the Canongate. Second Series [*St. Valentine's Day, or The Fair Maid of Perth*]. Edinburgh: Cadell and Company, 1829.

Anne of Geierstein, or The Maiden of the Mist. Edinburgh: Cadell and Company, 1829.

Tales of My Landlord. Fourth and Last Series [*Count Robert of Paris* and *Castle Dangerous*]. London: R. Cadell, 1832.

SECONDARY SOURCES

1. Books about Sir Walter Scott

ADOLPHUS, JOHN LEYCESTER. *Letters to Richard Heber, Esq. Containing Critical Remarks on the Series of Novels Beginning with "Waverley" and an Attempt to Ascertain Their Author.* London: Rodell and Martin, 1822. The first extended piece of Scott criticism. Discusses characteristics common to the poems and the novels.

BALL, MARGARET. *Sir Walter Scott as a Critic of Literature.* New York: Columbia University Press, 1907. A convenient summary of Scott's critical opinions.

BUCHAN, JOHN. *Sir Walter Scott.* London: Cassell and Company, 1932. Highly readable, wholeheartedly admiring biography, including considerable criticism.

CORSON, J. C. *A Bibliography of Scott: A Classified and Annotated List of Books and Articles Relating to His Life and Works, 1797–1940.* Edinburgh: Oliver & Boyd, 1943.

DAVIE, DONALD. *The Heyday of Sir Walter Scott.* New York: Barnes and Noble, 1961. Discusses the influence of Scott on Pushkin, Cooper, and Mickiewicz (nineteenth-century Lithuanian poet).

GRIERSON, H. J. C. *Sir Walter Scott, Bart.: A New Life Supplementary to, and Corrective of, Lockhart's Biography.* London: Constable and Company, 1938. A necessary corrective to Lockhart. Concerned primarily with Scott's business affairs, but includes some valuable brief criticisms.

—— and others. *Sir Walter Scott Lectures: 1940–1948.* Edinburgh:

The University Press, 1950. Admiring and conventional criticism, except for Edwin Muir's penetrating and not entirely sympathetic study of Scott's personality and its relation to his work.

HILLHOUSE, JAMES T. *The Waverley Novels and Their Critics*. Minneapolis: University of Minnesota Press, 1936. Valuable summary of critical opinion from 1814 to the time of publication.

LOCKHART, JOHN GIBSON. *Memoirs of the Life of Sir Walter Scott*. 5 vols. New York: Houghton Mifflin and Company, 1902. A compilation rather than a biography, including much material from Scott's letters and journals, and long quotations from contemporary reviews. Highly sympathetic (Lockhart was Scott's son-in-law) but untrustworthy. Facts sometimes altered or even invented.

PEARSON, HESKETH. *Sir Walter Scott: His Life and Personality*. London: Methuen, 1954. Sympathetic, gossipy, and readable. Critical judgments erratic, contains no new information.

WELSH, ALEXANDER. *The Hero of the Waverley Novels*. New Haven: Yale University Press, 1963. A thoughtful and stimulating discussion of the "passive hero," the "dark hero," and the motifs of honor, property, and anxiety in the novels.

2. Articles and sections of books discussing Scott. (This section is highly selective.)

BAGEHOT, WALTER. "The Waverley Novels," *Literary Studies*, II. London: Longmans, Green and Co., 1879. Representative Victorian criticism, praises Scott's soundness but deprecates the superficiality of his characterizations.

BLUNDEN, EDMUND. "The Poetry of Scott," *Queen's Quarterly*, XXXIX (November, 1932), 593–602. A witty but superficial survey.

COLERIDGE'S *Miscellaneous Criticism*. Ed. T. M. Raysor. Cambridge: Harvard University Press, 1936. Coleridge's scattered remarks include the most penetrating contemporary criticism of Scott and anticipate most future criticism.

CRAIG, DAVID. "*The Heart of Midlothian*: Its Religious Basis." *Essays in Criticism*, VIII (April, 1958), 217–25. Attempts to establish *The Heart of Midlothian* as a serious novel.

———. *Scottish Literature and the Scottish People, 1680–1830*. London: Chatto and Windus, 1961. Includes an informative and suggestive discussion of the social and linguistic difficulties facing Scottish writers in the early nineteenth century.

DAICHES, DAVID. "Scott's Achievement as a Novelist," *Nineteenth Century Fiction*, VI (September and December, 1951). Considers Scott's interpretation of the history of Scotland, and the conflict between glamorous past and prosaic present.

Selected Bibliography

————. "Scott's *Redgauntlet*," *From Jane Austen to Joseph Conrad: Essays in Memory of James T. Hillhouse*, ed. Robert C. Rathbun. Minneapolis: University of Minnesota Press, 1958. An interpretation of *Redgauntlet* as "Scott's *Don Quixote*."

DUNCAN, JOSEPH. "The Anti-Romantic in *Ivanhoe*," *Nineteenth Century Fiction*, IX (March, 1955), 293–300. Refutes the conventional opinion; similar to Daiches in approach.

FIEDLER, LESLIE A. *Love and Death in the American Novel*. New York: Criterion Books, 1960. Includes many suggestive (although sometimes farfetched) comments on the thematic significance of Scott's novels and their influence on American fiction.

FISHER, P. F. "Providence, Fate and the Historical Imagination in Scott's *The Heart of Midlothian*," *Nineteenth Century Fiction*, X (September, 1955), 99–114. A defense of the novel.

FORBES, DUNCAN. "The Rationalism of Sir Walter Scott," *The Cambridge Journal*, VII (October, 1953), 20–36. Sees Scott as essentially an eighteenth-century rationalist.

FORSTER, E. M. *Aspects of the Novel*. New York: Harcourt, Brace and Company, 1927. Includes the most devastating modern attack on Scott.

GORDON, S. STEWART. "*Waverley* and the 'Unified Design'," *English Literary History*, XVIII (March, 1951), 107–22. Attempts to demonstrate the artistic unity of *Waverley*.

HAZLITT, WILLIAM. "Why Heroes of Romance are Insipid," *Complete Works of William Hazlitt*, XVII. Ed. P. P. Howe. London: J. M. Dent and Sons, 1933. Principally an apology for the passive hero of the Waverley Novels.

JEFFREY, FRANCIS. Review of "Marmion: A Tale of Flodden Field," *Edinburgh Review*, XII (April, 1808), 1–36. A representative contemporary review of Scott's poetry.

KROEBER, KARL. "The Narrative Pattern of Scott." *Romantic Narrative Art*. Madison: University of Wisconsin Press, 1960. The most sympathetic and extended modern criticism of Scott's poetry. Sees it as preliminary to the novels.

LUKACS, GEORG. *The Historical Novel*. Translated by Hannah and Stanley Mitchell. London: Merlin Press, 1962. Surprisingly sympathetic criticism by a well-known Marxist. Primarily concerned with Scott's philosophy of history.

MAYHEAD, ROBIN. "*The Heart of Midlothian*: Scott as Artist," *Essays in Criticism*, VI (July, 1956), 266–77. A defense of the unity and seriousness of the novel.

STEVENSON, R. L. "A Gossip on Romance." *Memories and Portraits*.

New York: Charles Scribner & Sons, 1901. Sees Scott as a "dreamer" rather than an artist.

TILLYARD, E. M. W. "Scott's Linguistic Vagaries," *Etudes Anglaises,* XI (1958, 112–18. Discusses the peculiar mixture of idioms and dialects used by Scott in *The Monastery* and later novels.

VAN GHENT, DOROTHY. *"The Heart of Midlothian." The English Novel: Form and Function.* New York: Holt, Rinehart and Winston, 1953. A destructive analysis.

WOOLF, VIRGINIA. "Sir Walter Scott," *The Moment.* New York: Harcourt, Brace and Company, 1948. Defense of Scott against modern detractors.

Index

Index